Welcome Home
COZY DINNERS

Welcome Home
COZY DINNERS

QUICK & EASY FAMILY FAVORITES

Photos by Bonnie Matthews

New York, New York

Photos by Bonnie Matthews

Good Books books may be purchased in bulk at special discounts for sales promotion, corporate gifts, fund-raising, or educational purposes. Special editions can also be created to specifications. For details, contact the Special Sales Department, Good Books, 307 West 36th Street, 11th Floor, New York, NY 10018 or info@skyhorsepublishing.com.

Good Books is an imprint of Skyhorse Publishing, Inc.®, a Delaware corporation.

Visit our website at www.goodbooks.com.

10 9 8 7 6 5 4 3 2 1

Library of Congress Cataloging-in-Publication Data is available on file.

Cover design by Kai Texel
Cover photo by Bonnie Matthews

Print ISBN: 978-1-68099-975-4
Ebook ISBN: 978-1-964219-12-7

Printed in China

Table of Contents

About *Welcome Home Cozy Dinners*

Cozy on up to a delicious, easy, and home-cooked meal with the *Welcome Home Cozy Dinners* cookbook! Enjoy an incredible soup, amazing entree, or even breakfast for dinner, all made from the convenience of your oven, stovetop, slow cooker or Instant Pot. Finish off your meal with several delicious desserts to choose from. All 127 recipes are sure to make you feel warm from the inside-out!

As you begin journeying through this book, I always suggest reading it from cover to cover. I can't tell you the good recipes I've passed on in the past by not following this advice. Don't become overwhelmed. Bookmark or dog-ear the pages of the recipes that you think your family would enjoy the most, can be made with ingredients you have around the house, or fit with their dietary needs. Then, when you've looked at everything, go back to those marked pages and narrow it down. Make yourself a grocery list and grab what you don't already have. Voilà! You're ready to get cooking!

Breakfast for Dinner

Veggie Quiche

Hope Comerford, Clinton Township, MI

Makes 4–6 servings

Prep. Time: 25 minutes ❀ *Baking Time: 1 hour*

1 prepared piecrust
1 tsp. prepared mustard
½ cup chopped asparagus
½ cup chopped zucchini
½ cup chopped summer squash
½ cup chopped mushrooms
½ cup chopped onion
1 Tbsp. olive oil
10 oz. shredded Monterey Jack cheese
3–4 eggs
1 cup milk
1 tsp. garlic powder
1 tsp. onion powder
½ tsp. salt
½ tsp. pepper

1. Preheat the oven to 325°F.

2. Press the prepared crust into the bottom of a pie plate. Brush it with the prepared mustard.

3. Sauté the asparagus, zucchini, summer squash, mushrooms, and onion in the olive oil until they are tender. Place evenly into bottom of the pie crust, then sprinkle the cheese over the top.

4. In a bowl, beat the eggs with the milk, garlic powder, onion powder, salt, and pepper.

5. Pour the egg mixture into the prepared crust. Bake for 1 hour.

6. When the egg is set in the middle, the quiche is done. Let it cool for about 10 minutes before slicing and serving.

Turkey Bacon, Spinach, and Gruyère Quiche

Hope Comerford, Clinton Township, MI

Makes 4–6 servings

Prep. Time: 15 minutes ❧ *Cooking Time: 3–4 hours* ❧ *Ideal slow-cooker size: 6-qt.*

- 8 eggs
- 1 cup unsweetened almond milk
- 1 tsp. salt
- 1 tsp. pepper
- 1 tsp. garlic powder
- 1 tsp. onion powder
- ½ cup chopped onion
- 5 slices turkey bacon, diced
- 2 handfuls (about 2 oz.) fresh spinach leaves
- 8 oz. Gruyère cheese, shredded

1. In a bowl, mix the eggs, milk, salt, pepper, garlic powder, and onion powder. Pour this into the bottom of your greased crock.
2. Sprinkle the onion and bacon evenly over the surface of the eggs.
3. Spread the spinach all over the top of the egg mixture in your crock.
4. Cover the spinach with the shredded cheese.
5. Cover and cook on Low for 3–4 hours, or until it is completely set in the middle.

Breakfast Pie

Darlene Bloom, San Antonio, TX

Makes 6 servings

Prep. Time: 20 minutes ❧ *Baking Time: 30 minutes* ❧ *Standing Time: 5–10 minutes*

- 8 oz. lower-sodium ham
- 1 cup chopped onion
- 1 cup chopped bell pepper, red or green
- 1 cup 75%-less-fat shredded cheddar cheese
- ½ cup reduced-fat buttermilk baking mix
- 1 cup fat-free milk
- 2 eggs

1. Brown meat, onion, and bell pepper in skillet on stove until done. Drain off drippings.
2. Place cooked ingredients in a greased 9-inch pie plate.
3. Top with layer of shredded cheese.
4. In a mixing bowl, whisk baking mix, milk, and eggs together. Pour over ingredients in pie plate.
5. Bake at 400°F for 30 minutes.
6. Allow to stand 5–10 minutes before cutting and serving.

Tips:

1. Double this recipe and prepare in a 9 × 13-inch baking pan. I take this to potlucks all the time (warm) out of the oven.
2. You can use ground turkey or beef as your choice of meat and add 1 pkg. taco seasoning mix to the skillet as you cook. I call this version Taco Bake and often make it for dinner.

Shredded Potato Omelet

Mary H. Nolt, East Earl, PA

Makes 6 servings

Prep. Time: 15 minutes ✿ *Cooking Time: 20 minutes*

- 3 slices bacon, cooked and crumbled
- 2 cups shredded cooked potatoes
- 1/4 cup minced onion
- 1/4 cup minced green bell pepper
- 1 cup egg substitute
- 1/4 cup nonfat milk
- 1/4 tsp. salt
- 1/8 tsp. black pepper
- 1 cup 75%-less-fat shredded cheddar cheese
- 1 cup water

1. With nonstick cooking spray, spray the inside of a round baking dish that will fit in your Instant Pot inner pot.
2. Sprinkle the bacon, potatoes, onion, and bell pepper around the bottom of the baking dish.
3. Mix together the egg substitute, milk, salt, and pepper in mixing bowl. Pour over potato mixture.
4. Top with cheese.
5. Add water to the inner pot, place the steaming rack into the bottom of the inner pot, and place the round baking dish on top.
6. Close the lid and secure to the locking position. Be sure the vent is turned to sealing. Set for 20 minutes on Manual at high pressure.
7. Let the pressure release naturally.
8. Carefully remove the baking dish with the handles of the steaming rack and allow to stand for 10 minutes before cutting and serving.

Breakfast For Dinner Casserole

INSTANT POT

Hope Comerford, Clinton Township, MI

Makes 4–6 servings

Prep. Time: 15 minutes ❧ *Cooking Time: 25 minutes*

1 Tbsp. olive oil
½ lb. bulk breakfast sausage
½ cup finely diced onion
1 cup water
½ lb. frozen Tater Tots or hash browns
6 eggs
¼ cup half-and-half
½ tsp. salt
½ tsp. garlic powder
¼ tsp. black pepper
⅛ tsp. cayenne pepper
½ cup diced bell pepper (any color you wish)
1 cup shredded pepper Jack cheese
½ cup shredded cheddar cheese

1. Set the Instant Pot to the Sauté function and add the olive oil.

2. Add the bulk sausage and onion to the inner pot of the Instant Pot and cook until browned. Remove it from the Instant Pot and set aside. Press the Cancel button.

3. Carefully wipe out the inside of the Instant Pot. Pour in the water and scrape the bottom, to be sure there is nothing stuck. Place the trivet on top with handles up.

4. Grease a 7-inch baking pan with butter or nonstick cooking spray. Arrange the Tater Tots or hash browns evenly around the bottom of the pan.

5. In a bowl, mix the eggs, half-and-half, salt, garlic powder, black pepper, and cayenne. Stir in the bell pepper and pepper Jack cheese. Pour this over the hash browns.

6. Sprinkle the cheddar over the top of the casserole. Cover with foil. Carefully lower the baking pan onto the trivet.

7. Secure the lid and set the vent to sealing. Manually set the cook time for 25 minutes on high pressure.

8. When the cook time is over, let the pressure release naturally for 10 minutes, then manually release the remaining pressure.

9. With hot pads, carefully remove the baking pan with the handles of the trivet. Uncover, serve, and enjoy!

Variation:

You can use any types of cheese that your family likes. You do not have to stick with what is suggested above. Also, you could use bacon instead of sausage, or omit the meat altogether.

Overnight Breakfast Casserole

Hannah D. Burkholder, Bridgewater, VA
Esther S. Martin, Ephrata, PA

Makes 8–10 servings

Prep. Time: 45 minutes ❧ *Chilling Time: 8 hours, or overnight* ❧ *Baking Time: 1 hour*

1 lb. fresh bulk sausage
4 cups cubed day-old bread
2 cups shredded sharp cheddar cheese
1 tsp. dry mustard
10 eggs, slightly beaten
4 cups milk
1 tsp. salt
Freshly ground pepper to taste
¼ cup chopped or grated onion
½ cup peeled, chopped tomatoes, *optional*
½ cup diced green and red peppers, *optional*
½ cup sliced fresh mushrooms, *optional*

1. Cook the sausage in a skillet until browned. Drain and break up the meat into small pieces. Set aside.

2. Place bread in a buttered 9 × 13-inch baking dish. Sprinkle with cheese.

3. Combine the next six ingredients. Pour evenly over the bread and cheese.

4. Sprinkle cooked sausage and chopped tomatoes, peppers, and mushrooms (if using) over the top.

5. Cover and chill in refrigerator for 8 hours, or overnight.

6. Preheat oven to 325°F. Bake uncovered for 1 hour. Tent with foil if top begins to brown too quickly.

Gold Rush Brunch

Trish Dick, Ladysmith, WI

Makes 12 servings

Prep. Time: 2 hours · *Baking Time: 40–45 minutes* · *Standing Time: 10 minutes*

4 large potatoes, peeled or unpeeled
½ stick (4 Tbsp.) butter, *divided*
2 Tbsp. chopped onion
2 Tbsp. parsley
1 lb. sausage, ham, or bacon
8 eggs, beaten
1 lb. shredded cheddar cheese, divided

White sauce:

½ stick (4 Tbsp.) butter
¼ tsp. salt
1¾ cups milk
¼ cup cornstarch
1 cup sour cream, *optional*

1. Boil potatoes until just soft. Cool to room temperature. Then refrigerate until chilled through.
2. When potatoes are cold, grate.
3. Melt 2 Tbsp. butter in large skillet. Stir potatoes and onion into skillet. Cook until lightly browned. Toss in parsley.
4. Spread in well-greased 9 × 13-inch baking pan.
5. Brown sausage, ham, or bacon in same skillet. Drain off drippings.
6. Crumble over potato layer in baking pan.
7. Melt 2 Tbsp. butter in skillet. Pour eggs into skillet. Cook, stirring up from the bottom until eggs are scrambled and just set.
8. Layer eggs over meat.
9. Sprinkle with half of shredded cheese.
10. Make white sauce by melting 4 Tbsp. butter in saucepan.
11. Stir in salt, milk, and cornstarch. Stir continually with a wooden spoon until bubbly and thickened.
12. Remove from heat. Stir in sour cream if you wish.
13. Pour white sauce over egg layer in pan.
14. Sprinkle with remaining shredded cheese.
15. Bake at 350°F for 40 minutes. Insert knife blade in center. If it comes out clean, the dish is finished. If it doesn't, continue baking another 5 minutes. Test again with knife blade. Continue cooking—and testing— as needed.
16. Allow to stand 10 minutes before cutting and serving.

Breakfast Pizza

Jessica Hontz, Coatesville, PA

Makes 8 servings

Prep. Time: 10 minutes ❧ *Baking Time: 20–25 minutes*

- 10-oz. refrigerated pizza crust
- 8 eggs
- ¼ cup milk or cream
- 6 slices bacon, cooked crisp and crumbled
- 2 cups shredded cheddar, or Monterey Jack, cheese

1. Unroll pizza crust onto baking sheet.
2. Bake at 425°F for 10 minutes.
3. Whisk together eggs and milk in a large mixing bowl.
4. Cook in skillet until eggs start to congeal, about 3–4 minutes. Spoon onto crust.
5. Top with bacon and cheese.
6. Bake an additional 10 minutes until eggs are set and crust is golden brown.

Country Breakfast Pizza

Zoë Rohrer, Lancaster, PA

Makes 8–10 servings

Prep. Time: 25–30 minutes ❧ *Baking Time: 27 minutes*

2 Tbsp. butter
1 cup whole wheat pastry flour
⅔ cup + 2 Tbsp. all-purpose flour
1 Tbsp. flax meal, *optional*
2 tsp. baking powder
½ tsp. salt
¼ cup real maple syrup
Scant ½ cup milk
½ green pepper, diced
⅔ lb. bulk pork sausage
9 large eggs
1⅓ cups grated cheddar cheese, *divided*
Maple syrup, or ketchup, for serving

1. Place butter in a 9 × 13-inch baking dish. Place dish in oven set at 425°F. Keep an eye on butter, and when it's melted (about 5 minutes), take dish out of oven.
2. Meanwhile, in a good-sized bowl, mix flours, flax if you wish, baking powder, and salt.
3. Add maple syrup and milk. Stir to combine.
4. Knead a few minutes in bowl, or on countertop, to make a ball.
5. Press dough into buttered baking dish.
6. Bake 12 minutes at 425°F. Remove from the oven.
7. While crust is baking, brown sausage and peppers in skillet until pink is gone from meat and peppers are just tender. Stir frequently to break up meat. Place cooked meat and peppers on platter (reserve drippings in skillet) and keep warm.
8. Beat eggs in mixing bowl. Pour into drippings in skillet. Stir frequently.
9. Add ⅔ cup cheese while eggs are cooking.
10. When crust is done, top with sausage, then eggs, and then remaining cheese.
11. Bake 10 more minutes or until cheese is melted.
12. Serve immediately with maple syrup or ketchup.

Italian Sausage and Sweet Pepper Hash

Hope Comerford, Clinton Township, MI

Makes 6–8 servings

Prep. Time: 10 minutes  *Cooking Time: 6½ hours* *Ideal slow-cooker size: 4-qt.*

12-oz. pkg. Italian turkey sausage, cut lengthwise, then into ½-inch pieces

16 oz. frozen diced potatoes

1½ cups sliced sweet onion

1 yellow pepper, sliced

1 green pepper, sliced

1 red pepper, sliced

¼ cup melted butter

1 tsp. sea salt

½ tsp. pepper

½ tsp. dry thyme

½ tsp. dry parsley

½ cup shredded Swiss cheese

1. Spray crock with nonstick spray.

2. Place sausage, frozen potatoes, onion, and sliced peppers into crock.

3. Mix melted butter with salt, pepper, thyme, and parsley. Pour over contents of crock and stir.

4. Cover and cook on Low for 6 hours. Sprinkle with the Swiss cheese, then cover and cook for an additional 20 minutes, or until the cheese is melted.

Huevos Rancheros in Crock

Pat Bishop, Bedminster, PA

Makes 6 servings

Prep. Time: 25 minutes ✤ *Cooking Time: 2 hours* ✤ *Ideal slow-cooker size: 6-qt.*

- 3 cups gluten-free salsa, room temperature
- 2 cups cooked beans, drained, room temperature
- 6 eggs, room temperature
- Salt and pepper to taste
- ⅓ cup grated Mexican-blend cheese, *optional*
- 6 white corn tortillas, for serving

1. Mix salsa and beans in slow cooker.
2. Cook on High for 1 hour or until steaming.
3. With a spoon, make 6 evenly spaced dents in the salsa mixture; try not to expose the bottom of the crock. Break an egg into each dent.
4. Salt and pepper eggs. Sprinkle with cheese if you wish.
5. Cover and continue to cook on High until egg whites are set and yolks are as firm as you like them, approximately 20–40 minutes.
6. To serve, scoop out an egg with some beans and salsa. Serve with warm tortillas.

Breakfast Polenta with Bacon

Margaret W. High, Lancaster, PA

Makes 8–10 servings

Prep. Time: 20 minutes • *Cooking Time: 2½ hours* • *Ideal slow-cooker size: 5–6-qt.*

4 eggs, room temperature
2 cups whole milk, room temperature
2 cups stone-ground (coarse) cornmeal
⅔ cup shredded Parmesan cheese, *divided*
4 cups boiling water
½ cup cooked, diced bacon
2 Tbsp. finely diced onion
2 cups chopped fresh spinach
1 tsp. salt
Pepper to taste

1. In a large mixing bowl, beat eggs. Whisk in milk, cornmeal, and ⅓ cup Parmesan.
2. Whisk in boiling water.
3. Gently stir in bacon, onion, spinach, salt, and pepper.
4. Pour mixture into well-greased slow cooker.
5. Cover and cook on High for 2 hours, stirring once to be sure cornmeal is evenly distributed as it cooks.
6. When polenta is thick, sprinkle with remaining ⅓ cup Parmesan. Remove lid and allow to cook on High for an additional 30 minutes as cheese melts and any extra liquid evaporates. Polenta will be softer when hot, but will firm up as it cools. Serve hot, warm, or chilled.

Brunch Enchiladas

Ann Good, Perry, NY

Makes 10 servings

Prep. Time: 20–35 minutes · *Chilling Time: 8–12 hours* · *Baking Time: 45–60 minutes*

- ¾ cup chopped onion
- ¾ cup chopped bell peppers
- ½ stick (4 Tbsp.) butter
- 2 cups chopped cooked ham
- 2 cups cooked bulk sausage
- 16-oz. container sour cream
- 16 (8-inch) flour tortillas
- 4 cups shredded cheese, *divided*
- 16 eggs
- 1½ cups milk
- 2 Tbsp. flour
- ½ tsp. salt
- ½ tsp. pepper

1. In saucepan, sauté onion and peppers in butter until soft.
2. Stir in meat and cook until heated through.
3. Spread a strip of sour cream through the center of each tortilla.
4. Spoon ⅓ cup meat mixture on top of sour cream on each tortilla.
5. Top with ¼ cup cheese on each tortilla, using a total of 3 cups cheese.
6. Roll up and place seams down in two well-greased 9 × 13-inch baking pans.
7. In a large mixing bowl, beat together eggs, milk, flour, salt, and pepper.
8. Pour over tortillas. Cover. Refrigerate overnight.
9. Remove from refrigerator for 30 minutes before baking.
10. Bake uncovered at 350°F for 45–60 minutes, or until heated through.
11. Remove from oven. Sprinkle with remaining 1 cup cheese.
12. Let stand 5–10 minutes before serving.

Variations:

1. Serve with salsa and sour cream.
2. Top the just-baked enchiladas with thin slices of fresh tomatoes in Step 11 before sprinkling with cheese.

Tip:

This dish freezes well.

Cinnamon French Toast

Hope Comerford, Clinton Township, MI

Makes 8 servings

Prep. Time: 10 minutes ❧ *Cooking Time: 20 minutes*

3 eggs
2 cups milk
¼ cup maple syrup
1 tsp. vanilla extract
1 tsp. cinnamon
Pinch salt
16-oz. loaf cinnamon swirl bread, cubed and left out overnight to go stale
1 cup water

1. In a medium bowl, whisk together the eggs, milk, maple syrup, vanilla, cinnamon, and salt. Stir in the cubes of cinnamon swirl bread.
2. Spray the inside of a 7-inch round pan with nonstick cooking spray, then pour the bread mixture into the pan.
3. Place the trivet in the bottom of the inner pot, then pour in the water.
4. Make a foil sling and insert it onto the trivet. Carefully place the 7-inch pan on top of the foil sling/trivet.
5. Secure the lid to the locked position, then make sure the vent is turned to sealing.
6. Press the Manual button and use the "+/-" button to set the Instant Pot for 20 minutes.
7. When the cook time is over, let the Instant Pot release naturally for 5 minutes, then quick release the rest.

Serving suggestion:
Serve with whipped cream and fresh fruit on top, with an extra sprinkle of cinnamon.

Blueberry French Toast

Stacie Skelly, Millersville, PA

Makes 12 servings

Prep. Time: 30 minutes · *Chilling Time: 6–12 hours* · *Baking Time: 1 hour*

12–15 slices day-old bread
8-oz. pkg. cream cheese
1 cup frozen blueberries
12 eggs
2 cups milk
⅓ cup honey

Sauce:

1 cup sugar
2 Tbsp. cornstarch
1 cup water
1 cup blueberries

1. Grease 9 × 13-inch baking pan.
2. Cube bread and spread in pan.
3. Cube cream cheese. Distribute evenly over bread.
4. Sprinkle blueberries on top.
5. In a mixing bowl, blend eggs, milk, and honey.
6. Pour over pan contents.
7. Cover. Refrigerate 6–8 hours, or overnight.
8. Remove from refrigerator 30 minutes before baking.
9. Bake, covered, at 350°F for 30 minutes.
10. Uncover. Bake 30 more minutes. Serve with sauce.

To make sauce:

1. Mix sugar, cornstarch, and water in a saucepan. Bring to a boil.
2. Stir in blueberries.
3. Reduce heat, cooking until blueberries burst.
4. Serve warm over French toast.

Soups, Stews, Chilies & Chowders

Chicken

Chicken Barley Soup

Ida H. Goering, Dayton, VA

Makes 6 servings

Prep. Time: 20 minutes ❧ *Cooking Time: 1 hour*

- 6 cups low-sodium, fat-free chicken broth
- 1½ cups diced carrots
- 1 cup diced celery
- ½ cup chopped onion
- ¼ cup uncooked barley
- 2–3 cups (about 6 oz.) cooked and cut-up chicken
- 14½-oz. can diced tomatoes, no salt added, undrained
- ½ tsp. black pepper
- 1 bay leaf
- 2 Tbsp. chopped fresh parsley, or 2 tsp. dry parsley

1. Combine all ingredients except parsley in large kettle.
2. Cover and bring to boil.
3. Simmer, covered, for one hour. Stir occasionally.
4. Just before serving, remove bay leaf. Stir in parsley.

Chicken Noodle Soup

Mary Martins, Fairbank, IA

Makes 12 servings

Prep. Time: 1 hour · *Cooking Time: 3–3 1/2 hours*

- 4-lb. stewing chicken, skin removed and cut up
- 2 qt. water
- 2 (14½-oz.) cans low-fat, low-sodium chicken broth
- 5 celery ribs, coarsely chopped, *divided*
- 3 medium carrots, sliced, *divided*
- 2 medium onions, quartered, *divided*
- ⅔ cup coarsely chopped green bell pepper, *divided*
- ½ tsp. pepper
- 1 bay leaf
- 2 tsp. salt
- 8 oz. dry whole wheat noodles

1. In large stockpot, combine chicken, water, broth, half the celery, half the carrots, half the onions, half the green pepper, ½ tsp. pepper, and bay leaf. Bring to a boil.
2. Reduce heat. Cover and simmer 2½ hours, or until chicken is tender.
3. Remove chicken from broth. When cool enough to handle, remove meat from bones and cut into bite-sized pieces. Discard bones and skin. Set chicken aside. (This will equal about 3 lb. cooked meat.)
4. Strain broth and skim fat.
5. Return broth to pot. Add salt and remaining celery, carrots, onions, and green pepper.
6. Bring to a boil. Reduce heat. Cover and simmer 10–12 minutes, or until vegetables are crisp-tender.
7. Remove bay leaf. Add noodles and chicken.
8. Cover and simmer 12–15 minutes, or until pasta is tender.

Chicken Rice Soup

Unknown Author

Makes 8 servings

Prep. Time: 8 minutes · *Cooking Time: 4–8 hours* · *Ideal slow-cooker size: 4- or 6-qt.*

4 cups chicken broth
4 cups chopped cooked chicken
1⅓ cups chopped celery
1⅓ cups diced carrots
4 cups water
1 cup uncooked long-grain rice

1. Combine all ingredients in slow cooker.
2. Cover and cook on Low 4 to 8 hours or until vegetables are cooked to your liking.

Chicken and Vegetable Soup with Rice

Hope Comerford, Clinton Township, MI

Makes 6–8 servings

Prep. Time: 20 minutes ❧ *Cooking Time: 6½–7½ hours* ❧ *Ideal slow-cooker size: 3-qt.*

- 1½–2 lb. boneless, skinless chicken breasts
- 1½ cups chopped carrots
- 1½ cups chopped red onion
- 2 Tbsp. garlic powder
- 1 Tbsp. onion powder
- 2 tsp. kosher salt
- ¼ tsp. celery seed
- ¼ tsp. paprika
- ⅛ tsp. pepper
- 1 dry bay leaf
- 8 cups no-salt chicken stock
- 1 cup fresh green beans
- 3 cups cooked rice

1. Place chicken into the bottom of crock, then add rest of the remaining ingredients, except green beans and rice.

2. Cover and cook on Low for 6–7 hours.

3. Remove chicken and chop into bite-sized cubes. Place chicken back into crock and add in green beans. Cover and cook another 30 minutes.

4. To serve, place approximately ½ cup of the cooked rice into each bowl and ladle soup over top of the rice.

Easy Chicken Tortilla Soup

Becky Harder, Monument, CO

Makes 6–8 servings

Prep. Time: 5–10 minutes · *Cooking Time: 8 hours* · *Ideal slow-cooker size: 4- to 5-qt.*

- 4 chicken breast halves
- 2 (15-oz.) cans black beans, undrained
- 2 (15-oz.) cans Mexican stewed tomatoes, or Ro*Tel tomatoes
- 1 cup salsa (mild, medium, or hot, whichever you prefer)
- 4-oz. can chopped green chilies
- 14½-oz. can tomato sauce
- Tortilla chips

1. Combine all ingredients except tortilla chips in large slow cooker.

2. Cover. Cook on Low 8 hours.

3. Just before serving, remove chicken breasts and slice into bite-sized pieces. Stir into soup.

4. Put a handful of tortilla chips in each individual soup bowl. Ladle soup over chips. Top with shredded cheese.

Family Favorite Chicken Fajita Soup

Maria Shevlin, Sicklerville, NJ

Makes 10–12 servings

Prep. Time: 20 minutes · *Cooking Time: 5 minutes*

1 Tbsp. olive oil
1 medium onion, chopped
5 celery stalks, sliced down the center lengthwise, then chopped
4 cloves garlic, minced
1 cup frozen corn
5 cups chicken stock
2 cups water
32 oz. picante sauce (we love Pace)
¾ tsp. cumin
1 heaping Tbsp. chili powder
1 heaping Tbsp. paprika
½ cup celery leaves, chopped
4 cups precooked chicken (you can use a rotisserie chicken for this)
15-oz. can black beans, rinsed and drained
3 bell peppers, chopped

Optional toppings:

Green onion, chopped
Tortilla strips
Sour cream
Mexican blend or taco-flavored shredded cheese
Sliced jalapeños

1. Set the Instant Pot to the Sauté setting and let it get hot. Add the oil.
2. Sauté the onion, celery, and garlic for approximately 3–5 minutes.
3. Add the corn and mix well.
4. Stir in the chicken stock, water, picante sauce, and spices, including the celery leaves.
5. Add the precooked chicken, beans, and peppers, and mix well.
6. Secure the lid and set the vent to sealing. Manually set the cook time for 5 minutes on high pressure.
7. When cook time is up, manually release the pressure.
8. To serve, ladle into bowls and top with any, or all, of the optional toppings you want.

Chicken Taco Soup

Mary Puskar, Forest Hill, MD

Makes 4 servings

Prep. Time: 25 minutes ⁂ *Cooking Time: 40 minutes*

2 chicken breast halves
3 cups water
2 stalks celery
1 medium-sized onion
2 carrots
2 Tbsp. vegetable or canola oil
1 Tbsp. chili powder
1 Tbsp. cumin
4½-oz. can green chilies
14-oz. can chicken broth
14-oz. can beef broth
14½-oz. can diced tomatoes, undrained
1 Tbsp. Worcestershire sauce
Tortilla chips, broken
Monterey Jack cheese, grated

1. In a large stockpot, cook chicken breasts in water until tender. Remove meat, reserving cooking water. When chicken is cool enough to handle, chop into bite-sized pieces. Set aside.

2. Chop celery and onion. Grate carrots.

3. In stockpot used for cooking chicken, sauté vegetables in oil.

4. Combine all ingredients in stockpot, except the cooked chicken, tortilla chips, and cheese. Cover and simmer 15 minutes.

5. Add diced chicken. Heat through.

6. Top each serving with broken tortilla chips and grated cheese.

Chicken Tortellini Soup

Mary Seielstad, Sparks, NV

Makes 4–6 servings

Prep. Time: 10–15 minutes ✿ *Cooking Time: 25 minutes*

1 Tbsp. butter or margarine
4 cloves garlic, minced
5 cups chicken broth
9-oz. pkg. frozen cheese tortellini
1½ cups diced cooked chicken
14-oz. can stewed tomatoes
10-oz. pkg. frozen spinach
½ tsp. pepper
1 tsp. dry basil
¼ cup grated Parmesan cheese

1. In large saucepan, melt butter and sauté garlic for 2 minutes over medium heat.

2. Stir in broth and tortellini and bring to a boil. Cover, reduce heat, and simmer 5 minutes.

3. Add cooked chicken, tomatoes, frozen spinach, pepper, and basil and simmer 10–15 minutes. Stir every 3 minutes or so, breaking up frozen spinach and blending it into the soup.

4. Serve when soup is heated through, along with Parmesan cheese to spoon over individual servings.

Creamy Chicken Wild Rice Soup

Vonnie Oyer, Hubbard, OR

Makes 4–6 servings

Prep. Time: 15 minutes *Cooking Time: 15 minutes*

2 Tbsp. butter
½ cup diced yellow onion
¾ cup diced carrots
¾ cup sliced mushrooms (about 3–4 mushrooms)
½ lb. chicken breast, diced into 1-inch cubes
6.2-oz. box Uncle Ben's Long Grain & Wild Rice Fast Cook
2 (14-oz.) cans chicken broth
1 cup milk
1 cup half-and-half
2 oz. cream cheese
2 Tbsp. cornstarch

1. Select the Sauté feature and add the butter, onion, carrots, and mushrooms to the inner pot. Sauté for about 5 minutes until onions are translucent and soft.

2. Add the cubed chicken and seasoning packet from the Uncle Ben's box and stir to combine.

3. Add the wild rice and chicken broth. Select Manual, high pressure, then lock the lid and make sure the vent is set to sealing. Set the time for 5 minutes.

4. After the cooking time ends, allow it to stay on Keep Warm for 5 minutes and then quick release the pressure.

5. Remove the lid; change the setting to the Sauté function again.

6. Add the milk, half-and-half, and cream cheese. Stir to melt.

7. In a small bowl, mix the cornstarch with a little bit of water to dissolve, then add to the soup to thicken.

INSTANT POT

Chicken Cheddar Broccoli Soup

Maria Shevlin, Sicklerville, NJ

Makes 4–6 servings

Prep. Time: 15 minutes ꕥ *Cooking Time: 15 minutes* ꕥ *Recommended Instant Pot Size: 6-qt.*

- 1 lb. raw chicken breast, thinly chopped/sliced
- 1 lb. fresh broccoli, chopped
- ½ cup onion, chopped
- 2 cloves garlic, minced
- 1 cup shredded carrots
- ½ cup finely chopped celery
- ¼ cup finely chopped red bell pepper
- 3 cups chicken bone broth
- ½ tsp. salt
- ¼ tsp. black pepper
- ½ tsp. garlic powder
- 1 tsp. parsley flakes
- Pinch red pepper flakes
- 2 cups heavy cream
- 8 oz. freshly shredded cheddar cheese
- 2 Tbsp. Frank's RedHot Original Cayenne Pepper Sauce

1. Place chicken, broccoli, chopped onion, garlic, carrots, celery, bell pepper, chicken broth, and seasonings in the pot and stir to mix.
2. Secure the lid and make sure vent is at sealing. Place on Manual at high pressure for 15 minutes.
3. Manually release the pressure when cook time is up, remove lid, and stir in heavy cream.
4. Place pot on sauté setting until it all comes to a low boil, approximately 5 minutes.
5. Stir in cheese and the hot sauce.
6. Turn off the pot as soon as you add the cheese and give it a stir.
7. Continue to stir until the cheese is melted.

Serving suggestion:

Serve it up with slice or two of garlic bread or bread of your choice.

Chicken Stew

Hope Comerford, Clinton Township, MI

Makes 6 servings

Prep. Time: 10 minutes ❧ *Cooking Time: 20 minutes*

1 Tbsp. olive oil
1 cup chopped onion
3 carrots, chopped
2 celery stalks, chopped
4 cups chicken broth, *divided*
2 lb. boneless, skinless chicken breasts, diced
4–5 red potatoes, chopped
2½ tsp. salt
3 tsp. garlic powder
3 tsp. onion powder
1½ tsp. Italian seasoning
¼ tsp. pepper
2 bay leaves
2 Tbsp. cornstarch
2 Tbsp. cold water

1. Press Sauté on the Instant Pot. Let it get hot. Add the oil.

2. Sauté the onion, carrots, and celery for about 3–5 minutes.

3. Pour in 1 cup of the broth and scrape the bottom of the inner pot to bring up any stuck-on bits. Press Cancel.

4. Add the chicken, red potatoes, salt, garlic powder, onion powder, Italian seasoning, pepper, bay leaves, and remaining 3 cups of broth.

5. Secure the lid and set the vent to sealing. Manually set the cook time for 10 minutes on high pressure.

6. When cook time is up, let the pressure release naturally for 10 minutes, then manually release the remaining pressure. When the pin drops, remove the lid. Press Cancel.

7. Press the Sauté function once again. Mix the cornstarch and cold water, then stir it into the stew. Let it simmer for about 5 minutes, or until it is thickened. Remove the bay leaves before serving.

Tip:

My family loves stew with crusty Italian or French bread with butter on top.

White Chicken Chili

Hope Comerford, Clinton Township, MI

Makes 4–6 servings

Prep. Time: 5 minutes *Cooking Time: 14 minutes*

2 cans great northern beans, undrained
1 large sweet onion, chopped
16-oz. jar of your favorite salsa
1 Tbsp. cumin
1 tsp. sea salt
¼ tsp. pepper
2 cups chicken stock
2 lb. boneless, skinless chicken breasts
8 oz. shredded pepper Jack cheese
8 oz. shredded Monterey Jack cheese

1. Place the beans, chopped onion, salsa, cumin, salt, pepper, and chicken stock into the inner pot of the Instant Pot, then place the chicken on top.

2. Secure the lid and set the vent to sealing. Manually set the cook time for 14 minutes on high pressure.

3. When cook time is up, manually release the pressure. When the pin drops, remove the lid.

4. Remove the chicken breasts and shred the meat between two forks. Stir it back through the contents of the inner pot, along with the shredded pepper Jack and Monterey Jack cheeses.

Serving suggestion:

This is very good with slices of avocado and crushed tortilla chips on top.

Chipotle Chili

Janie Steele, Moore, OK

Makes 6–8 servings

Prep. Time: 30 minutes ⁂ *Cooking Time: 3–6 hours* ⁂ *Ideal slow-cooker size: 3 4 qt.*

- 2 cloves garlic, chopped
- 1¼ lb. boneless, skinless chicken thighs, cubed
- 1 lb. butternut squash, peeled and cubed
- 15-oz. can pinto beans, rinsed and drained
- Juice and zest of ½ an orange
- 2–3 chipotle peppers in adobo sauce, minced
- 2 Tbsp. tomato paste
- 2 green onions, sliced
- Chopped cilantro, *optional*

1. Combine garlic, chicken, squash, beans, orange juice, orange zest, peppers, and tomato paste in slow cooker.

2. Cook 3–4 hours on High or 5–6 hours on Low, until chicken is done.

3. Mash some of the stew with potato masher to make it thicker.

4. Stir in green onions and optional cilantro. Serve hot.

Variation:

Use zest and juice of 1 lime instead of the orange.

Curried Chicken Chowder

Unknown Author

Makes 6–8 servings

Prep. Time: 8 minutes & *Cooking Time: 6 hours 25 minutes – 8 hours 25 minutes*
Ideal slow-cooker size: 4-qt.

- 2 chicken leg quarters, skinned
- 1 onion, chopped
- 1 cup chopped celery, leaves included
- 1 medium potato, diced
- 3 carrots, sliced
- 1 cup frozen green beans
- 1½ tsp. salt
- 1 Tbsp. curry powder, *divided*
- 1 bay leaf
- 5 cups water
- 1 apple, peeled and diced
- 3 Tbsp. all-purpose flour
- ⅓ cup half-and-half at room temperature
- Chopped fresh parsley for garnish

1. Place chicken in slow cooker. Add chopped onion, celery, potato, carrots, green beans, salt, 1½ teaspoons curry powder, and bay leaf. Pour 5 cups water over vegetables.

2. Cover and cook on Low 6 to 8 hours.

3. Remove chicken. Add diced apple and remaining 1½ teaspoons curry powder.

4. Remove chicken from bones and return meat to slow cooker.

5. Whisk together flour and half-and-half in a small bowl until completely smooth. Whisk into hot soup. Cover and cook on low 25 minutes more, stirring once or twice, until mixture is thick and apple is softened. Remove bay leaf before serving. Garnish, if desired.

Pork

The Best Bean and Ham Soup

Hope Comerford, Clinton Township, MI

Makes 8–10 servings

Prep. Time: 8 minutes ⁂ *Soaking Time: 8 hours or overnight*
Cooking Time: 8–12 hours ⁂ *Ideal slow-cooker size: 7-qt.*

1 lb. dry navy beans
1 meaty ham bone or shank
1 cup chopped onion
2 cloves garlic, minced
1 cup chopped celery
¼ cup chopped parsley
1 Tbsp. sea salt
1 tsp. pepper
1 tsp. nutmeg
1 tsp. oregano
1 tsp. basil
2 bay leaves
8 cups low-sodium chicken stock
6–8 cups water

1. Soak the navy beans in water for 8 hours. Make sure the water is at least 2–3 inches above the beans. Drain and rinse.

2. Place the ham bone in the bottom of the crock and pour all the remaining ingredients into the crock around it, ending with the water. You'll want to make sure you've covered the ham bone with water.

3. Cover and cook on Low for 8–12 hours.

Broccoli Rabe and Sausage Soup

Carlene Horne, Bedford, NH

Makes 4 servings

Prep. Time: 15 minutes ∗ *Cooking Time: 15 minutes*

- 2 Tbsp. olive oil
- 1 onion, chopped
- 1 lb. sweet or spicy sausage, casing removed, sliced
- 1 bunch broccoli rabe, approximately 5 cups chopped
- 32-oz. chicken broth
- 1 cup water
- 8 oz. frozen tortellini

1. Heat olive oil in a soup pot.
2. Add onion and sausage and sauté until tender.
3. Add broccoli rabe and sauté a few more minutes.
4. Pour broth and water into pan; bring to simmer.
5. Add tortellini and cook a few minutes until tender.

Variation:

Substitute any green such as Swiss chard, kale, or spinach for the broccoli rabe.

Serving suggestion:

Serve with grated cheese and crusty bread.

Split Pea Soup

Judy Gascho, Woodburn, OR

Makes 3–4 servings

Prep. Time: 20 minutes · *Cooking Time: 15 minutes*

- 4 cups chicken broth
- 4 sprigs thyme
- 4 oz. ham, diced (about ⅓ cup)
- 2 Tbsp. butter
- 2 celery stalks
- 2 carrots
- 1 large leek
- 3 cloves garlic
- 1½ cups dry green split peas (about 12 oz.)
- Salt and pepper to taste

1. Pour the broth into the inner pot of the Instant Pot and set to Sauté. Add the thyme, ham, and butter.

2. While the broth heats, chop the celery and cut the carrots into ½-inch-thick rounds. Halve the leek lengthwise and thinly slice. Chop the garlic. Add the vegetables to the pot as you cut them. Rinse the split peas in a colander, discarding any small stones, then add to the pot.

3. Secure the lid, making sure the steam valve is in the sealing position. Set the cooker to Manual at high pressure for 15 minutes. When the time is up, carefully turn the steam valve to the venting position to release the pressure manually.

4. Turn off the Instant Pot. Remove the lid and stir the soup; discard the thyme sprigs.

5. Thin the soup with up to 1 cup water if needed (the soup will continue to thicken as it cools). Season with salt and pepper.

Potato Soup

Michele Ruvola, Vestal, NY

Makes 4 servings

Prep. Time: 20 minutes *Cooking Time: 5 minutes*

5 lb. russet potatoes, peeled and cubed
3 celery stalks, sliced thin
1 large onion, diced
1 clove garlic, minced
1 Tbsp. seasoning salt
1 tsp. ground black pepper
½ stick (4 Tbsp.) butter
1 lb. bacon, fried crisp, rough chopped
4 cups chicken stock
1 cup heavy cream
½ cup whole milk

Optional garnishes:

Sour cream
Shredded cheddar cheese
Sliced green onions

1. Put potatoes, celery, onion, garlic, seasoning salt, pepper, and butter in the inner pot of the Instant Pot. Stir to combine.
2. Add bacon and chicken stock, then stir to combine.
3. Secure the lid and make sure the vent is on sealing. Push the Manual mode button, then set timer for 5 minutes on high pressure.
4. Quick release the steam when cook time is up.
5. Remove lid; mash potatoes to make a semismooth soup.
6. Add cream and milk; stir to combine.
7. Serve with garnishes if desired.

Serving suggestion:

Perfect on a cold night with slices of bread on the side or a salad.

Baked Potato Soup

Flo Quint, Quinter, KS
Susan Nafziger, Canton, KS

Makes 6–8 servings

Prep. Time: 30 minutes ❧ *Cooking Time: 15–20 minutes*

- 1½ sticks (12 Tbsp.) butter
- ⅔ cup flour
- 7 cups milk
- 4 cups baked potatoes (about 5 large potatoes), peeled and cubed
- 4 green onions, sliced thin
- 8–12 strips bacon (according to your taste preference), cooked and crumbled
- 1¼ cups shredded cheese
- 8 oz. sour cream, *optional*
- ¾ tsp. salt, *optional*
- ¼ tsp. pepper, *optional*

1. Melt butter in large stockpot. Add flour and stir until smooth over medium heat.
2. Add milk, stirring often until thickened. Be careful not to scorch.
3. Add potatoes and onions and bring to a boil. Reduce heat and simmer 5 minutes, stirring often.
4. Remove from heat and add bacon, cheese, and sour cream if desired. Stir until melted.
5. Add seasonings if desired and blend thoroughly.

Variation:

Instead of 7 cups milk, you can use 4 cups milk and 3 cups chicken broth.

Sausage and Kale Chowder

Beverly Hummel, Fleetwood, PA

Makes 6 servings

Prep. Time: 20 minutes · *Cooking Time: 5 hours* · *Ideal slow-cooker size: 4- to 5-qt.*

1 lb. bulk sausage
1 cup chopped onion
6 small red potatoes, chopped
1 cup thinly sliced kale, ribs removed
6 cups chicken broth
1 cup milk, at room temperature
Salt and pepper to taste

1. Brown sausage. Drain off grease. Transfer sausage to slow cooker.
2. Add onion, potatoes, kale, and broth.
3. Cook on High for 4 hours, until potatoes and kale are soft.
4. Add milk and cook on Low for 1 hour. Season to taste with salt and pepper.

Serving suggestion:

Italian bread and salad make a great accompaniment to this chowder.

Tip:

If you prefer a thicker soup, add 2 Tbsp. cornstarch to milk in Step 4 before adding to cooker. Stir several times in the last hour as chowder thickens.

Italian Shredded Pork Stew

Emily Fox, Bernville, PA

Makes 6–8 servings

Prep. Time: 20 minutes ❧ *Cooking Time: 8–10 hours* ❧ *Ideal slow-cooker size: 5-qt.*

- 2 medium sweet potatoes, peeled and cubed
- 2 cups chopped fresh kale
- 1 large onion, chopped
- 3 cloves garlic, minced
- 2½–3½ lb. boneless pork shoulder butt roast
- 14-oz. can white kidney or cannellini beans, drained
- 1½ tsp. Italian seasoning
- ½ tsp. salt
- ½ tsp. pepper
- 3 (14½-oz.) cans chicken broth
- Sour cream, *optional*

1. Place first four ingredients in slow cooker.
2. Place roast on vegetables.
3. Add beans and seasonings.
4. Pour the broth over top.
5. Cover and cook on Low 8–10 hours or until meat is tender.
6. Remove meat. Skim fat from cooking juices if desired. Shred pork with two forks and return to cooker. Heat through.
7. Garnish with sour cream if desired.

Beef

Beef Vegetable Soup

Anona M. Teel, Bangor, PA

Makes 6 servings

Prep. Time: 15 minutes ❧ *Cooking Time: 8–10 hours* ❧ *Ideal slow-cooker size: 6½-qt.*

1–1½-lb. soup bone
1 lb. stewing beef cubes
1½ qt. cold water
1 Tbsp. salt
¾ cup diced celery
¾ cup diced carrots
¾ cup diced potatoes
¾ cup diced onion
1 cup frozen mixed vegetables of your choice
16-oz. can diced tomatoes
⅛ tsp. pepper
1 Tbsp. chopped dry parsley

1. Put all ingredients in slow cooker.

2. Cover. Cook on Low 8–10 hours. Remove bone before serving.

Minestrone Soup

Lydia Konrad, Edmonton, Alberta

Makes 12 servings, about ¾ cup per serving

Prep. Time: 15 minutes ❧ *Cooking Time: about 2 hours*

1½ lb. 90%-lean ground beef
1 cup diced onion
1 cup diced zucchini
1 cup cubed potatoes
1 cup sliced carrots
½ cup diced celery
1 cup shredded cabbage
15-oz. can tomatoes, chopped
1½ qt. water
1 bay leaf
½ tsp. dry thyme
2 tsp. salt
Pepper to taste
1 tsp. Worcestershire sauce
¼ cup uncooked brown rice
½ cup freshly grated Parmesan cheese
Brown bread

1. Brown ground beef in large soup kettle. Drain off grease.

2. Add vegetables, water, seasonings, and Worcestershire sauce and bring to a boil.

3. Sprinkle rice into mixture. Cover and simmer for at least 1 hour.

4. Remove bay leaf. Sprinkle with Parmesan cheese and serve with brown bread.

Pasta Fagioli

Stacie Skelly, Millersville, PA

Makes 8–10 servings

Prep. Time: 20 minutes *Cooking Time: 1½ hours*

1 lb. ground beef
1 cup diced onion
1 cup julienned carrots
1 cup chopped celery
2 cloves garlic, minced
2 (14½-oz.) cans diced tomatoes, undrained
15-oz. can red kidney beans, undrained
15-oz. can great northern beans, undrained
15-oz. can tomato sauce
12-oz. can V8 juice
1 Tbsp. vinegar
1½ tsp. salt
1 tsp. dry oregano
1 tsp. dry basil
½ tsp. pepper
½ tsp. dry thyme
½ lb. dry ditali pasta

1. Brown ground beef in a large stockpot. Drain off drippings.

2. To browned beef, add onion, carrots, celery, and garlic. Sauté for 10 minutes.

3. Add remaining ingredients, except pasta, and stir well. Simmer, covered, for 1 hour.

4. About 50 minutes into cooking time, cook pasta in a separate saucepan, according to the directions on the package.

5. Add drained pasta to the large pot of soup. Simmer for 5–10 minutes and serve.

Tip:

If you can't find these short pasta tubes, you can substitute elbow macaroni.

Hearty Beef Barley Soup

Karen Gingrich, New Holland, PA

Makes 4–5 servings

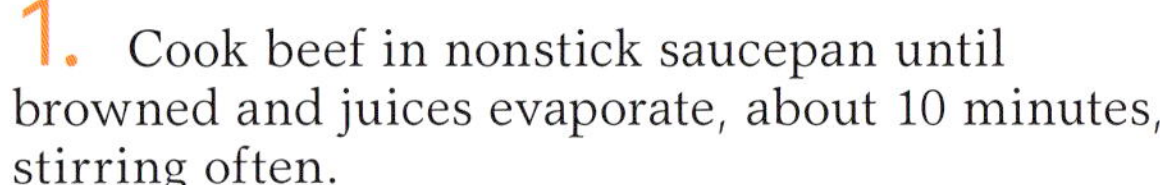

1 lb. beef tips
2 cups sliced fresh mushrooms
¼ tsp. garlic powder
32-oz. can (3½ cups) beef broth
2 medium-sized carrots, sliced
¼ tsp. dry thyme
Dash pepper
½ cup quick-cooking barley

1. Cook beef in nonstick saucepan until browned and juices evaporate, about 10 minutes, stirring often.

2. Add mushrooms and garlic powder and cook until mushrooms begin to wilt, about 5 minutes.

3. Add broth, carrots, thyme, and pepper.

4. Heat to boiling. Stir in barley. Cover and cook over low heat for 20 minutes, or until barley is tender.

Stuffed Sweet Pepper Soup

Moreen Weaver, Bath, NY

Makes 10 servings

Prep. Time: 20 minutes ∴ *Cooking Time: 1 hour*

- 1 lb. 95%-lean ground beef
- 2 qt. low-sodium tomato juice
- 3 medium red, or green, bell peppers, diced
- 1½ cups chili sauce, no salt added
- 1 cup uncooked brown rice
- 2 celery ribs, diced
- 1 large onion, diced
- 3 low-sodium chicken bouillon cubes
- 2 cloves garlic, minced

1. In large kettle over medium heat, cook beef until no longer pink. Drain off drippings.
2. Add remaining ingredients. Bring to a boil.
3. Reduce heat. Simmer, uncovered, for 1 hour, or until rice is tender.

Meatball Tortellini Soup

Lucille Amos, Greensboro, NC

Makes 4 servings

Prep. Time: 5 minutes ✤ *Cooking Time: 20–25 minutes*

14-oz. can beef broth
12 frozen Italian meatballs
1 cup stewed tomatoes
11-oz. can Mexican-style corn, drained
1 cup (20) frozen cheese tortellini

1. Bring broth to boil in a large stockpot.
2. Add meatballs. Cover and reduce heat. Simmer 5 minutes.
3. Add tomatoes and corn. Cover and simmer 5 minutes more.
4. Add tortellini. Cover and simmer 5 more minutes, or until tortellini is tender.

Hearty Beef Stew

Hope Comerford, Clinton Township, MI

Makes 6–8 servings

Prep. Time: 30 minutes · *Cooking Time: about 2 hours*

- 1½ lb. stew beef
- 1 Tbsp. olive oil
- 4–5 carrots, chopped
- 4 stalks celery, chopped
- 1 large onion, chopped
- 4 small- or medium-sized potatoes, diced
- 14½- oz. can diced tomatoes
- 6-oz. can tomato paste
- 7 cups beef stock
- 1 tsp. onion powder
- 1 tsp. salt
- 1 tsp. pepper
- 1 tsp. oregano
- 2 bay leaves

1. Lightly brown the stew beef in 1 Tbsp. olive oil in the bottom of a stew pot.
2. Add in the carrots, celery, and onion and cook until the onion is translucent.
3. Add in the potatoes, diced tomatoes, tomato paste, beef stock, onion powder, salt, pepper, oregano, and bay leaves. Stir well.
4. Bring to a boil.
5. Reduce to a simmer and cover. Cook for an additional 2 hours. Remove bay leaves before serving.

Slow-Cooker Beef Stew

Becky Fixel, Grosse Pointe Farms, MI

Makes 8–10 servings

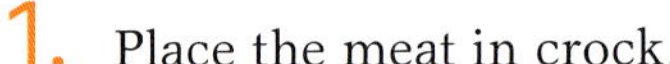

Prep. Time: 30 minutes ⁂ *Cooking Time: 6 hours* ⁂ *Ideal slow-cooker size: 3-qt.*

- 2 lb. cubed stew beef
- ¼ cup white rice flour
- 1½ tsp. salt
- ½ tsp. black pepper
- 32 oz. beef broth
- 1 onion, diced
- 1 tsp. Worcestershire sauce
- 1 bay leaf
- 1 tsp. paprika
- 4 carrots, sliced
- 3 potatoes, sliced thinly
- 1 stalk celery, sliced

1. Place the meat in crock.
2. Mix the flour, salt, and pepper. Pour over the meat and mix well. Make sure to cover the meat with flour.
3. Add broth to the crock and stir well.
4. Add remaining ingredients and stir to mix well.
5. Cook on High for at least 5 hours, then on Low for 1 hour. Remove bay leaf and serve.

Instantly Good Beef Stew

Hope Comerford, Clinton Township, MI

Makes 6 servings

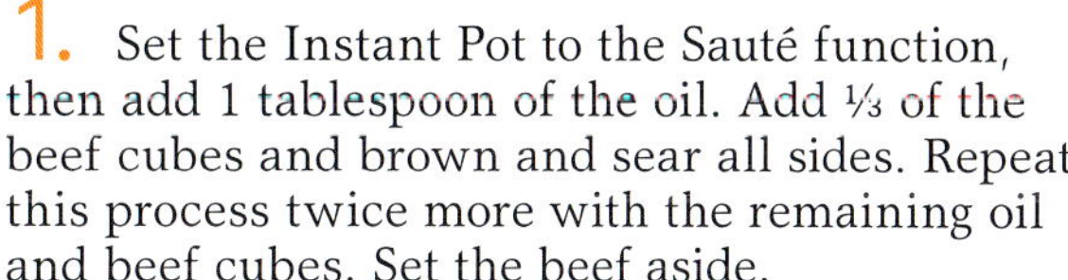

Prep. Time: 20 minutes ❧ *Cooking Time: 35 minutes*

3 Tbsp. olive oil, *divided*
2 lb. stewing beef, cubed
2 cloves garlic, minced
1 large onion, chopped
3 celery stalks, sliced
3 large potatoes, cubed
2–3 carrots, sliced
8 oz. no-salt-added tomato sauce
10 oz. low-sodium beef broth
2 tsp. Worcestershire sauce
¼ tsp. pepper
1 bay leaf

1. Set the Instant Pot to the Sauté function, then add 1 tablespoon of the oil. Add ⅓ of the beef cubes and brown and sear all sides. Repeat this process twice more with the remaining oil and beef cubes. Set the beef aside.

2. Place the garlic, onion, and celery into the pot and sauté for a few minutes. Press Cancel.

3. Add the beef back in as well as all the remaining ingredients.

4. Secure the lid and make sure the vent is set to sealing. Choose Manual for 35 minutes.

5. When cook time is up, let the pressure release naturally for 15 minutes, then release any remaining pressure manually.

6. Remove the lid, remove the bay leaf, then serve.

Tip:

If you want your stew to be a bit thicker, remove some of the potatoes, mash, then stir them back through the stew.

Meatball Stew

Hope Comerford, Clinton Township, MI

Makes 6–8 servings

Prep. Time: 30 minutes *Cooking Time: 2¼ hours*

Meatballs:

2 lb. lean ground beef
2 eggs
1–1½ cups breadcrumbs
1 Tbsp. dry minced onion
1 Tbsp. garlic powder
1 tsp. salt
¼ tsp. pepper
2–4 Tbsp. olive oil

Stew:

2 potatoes, peeled and cubed
4 carrots, peeled and sliced
1 large onion, chopped
4 cups green beans, cut into ½-inch pieces
1 cup chopped tomatoes
10-oz. can tomato sauce
10 cups water

1. Mix all the meatball ingredients except the olive oil. Form the meatball mixture into 1-inch balls.

2. Heat up the olive oil and brown the meatballs in batches just until the sides are slightly browned.

3. Set the meatballs aside.

4. In a large stockpot, place all the potatoes, carrots, onion, green beans, and chopped tomatoes. Add in the meatballs.

5. Pour in the can of tomato sauce, then the water. Stir gently.

6. Bring the soup to a boil, then reduce the heat to low and let it simmer for 2 hours.

Note:

While this takes a little bit of time to prepare, the effort is worth it! It is one of my most favorite "cozy meals!"

Our Favorite Chili

Ruth Shank, Gridley, IL

Makes 10–12 servings

Prep. Time: 20 minutes · *Cooking Time: 4–10 hours* · *Ideal slow-cooker size: 5-qt.*

- 1½ lb. extra-lean ground beef
- ¼ cup chopped onion
- 1 stalk celery, chopped
- Extra-virgin olive oil, *optional*
- 29-oz. can stewed tomatoes
- 2 (15½-oz.) cans red kidney beans, drained, rinsed
- 2 (16-oz.) cans chili beans, undrained
- ½ cup ketchup
- 1½ tsp. lemon juice
- 2 tsp. vinegar
- 1 tsp. brown sugar
- 1½ tsp. kosher salt
- 1 tsp. Worcestershire sauce
- ½ tsp. garlic powder
- ½ tsp. dry mustard powder
- 1 Tbsp. chili powder
- 2 (6-oz.) cans tomato paste

1. Brown ground beef, onion, and celery in oil (if using) in skillet. Stir frequently to break up clumps of meat. When meat is no longer pink, drain off drippings.

2. Place meat and vegetables in slow cooker. Add all remaining ingredients. Mix well.

3. Cover. Cook on Low 8–10 hours or on High 4–5 hours.

Southwestern Chili

Colleen Heatwole, Burton, MI

Makes 12 servings

Prep. Time: 30 minutes ❧ *Cooking Time: 6–8 hours* ❧ *Ideal slow-cooker size: 6- or 7-qt.*

32-oz. can whole tomatoes
15-oz. jar salsa
15-oz. can low-sodium chicken broth
1 cup barley
3 cups water
1 tsp. chili powder
1 tsp. ground cumin
15-oz. can black beans
15-oz. can whole kernel corn
3 cups chopped cooked chicken
1 cup low-fat shredded cheddar cheese, *optional*
Low-fat sour cream, *optional*

1. Combine all ingredients in slow cooker except for cheese and sour cream.

2. Cover and cook on Low for 6–8 hours.

3. Serve with cheese and sour cream on each bowl, if desired.

Beef and Bacon Chowder

Joan Dietrich, Kutztown, PA

Makes 8–10 servings

Prep. Time: 45 minutes · *Cooking Time: 1 hour*

12 bacon strips, cut in 1-inch pieces
1 lb. ground beef
2–3 cups diced celery
½ cup diced onion
2 (10¾-oz.) cans condensed cream of mushroom soup
4 cups milk
3–4 cups diced, cooked potatoes
2 cups shredded carrots
2 tsp. salt
1 tsp. pepper

1. In a large soup pot, cook bacon until crisp; pour off drippings and rcmovc bacon to paper towel to drain.

2. In the same pot, sauté ground beef with celery and onion until the beef is browned and the vegetables are tender. Drain off the grease.

3. Add soup, milk, potatoes, carrots, salt, and pepper.

4. Bring to a boil; reduce heat and simmer until heated through.

5. Add bacon.

Meatless

Chantal
Chantal

Fresh Vegetable Soup

Sandra Chang, Derwood, MD

Makes 4–6 servings

Prep. Time: 25–30 minutes · *Cooking Time: 60–70 minutes* · *Standing Time: 1 hour*

- 4 Tbsp. butter
- ½ cup diced celery
- ½ cup diced onion
- ½ cup small chunks of peeled carrots
- ½ cup chopped cabbage
- ½ cup diced zucchini
- ½ cup fresh or frozen whole kernel corn
- ½ cup fresh or frozen cut-up green beans
- 2 cups canned whole tomatoes
- 4 cups beef stock
- 2 Tbsp. sugar
- Salt and pepper to taste
- ½ cup fresh or frozen petite peas

1. In 4-qt. saucepan, melt butter. Sauté celery, onion, carrots, cabbage, and zucchini in butter until vegetables are soft but not brown.
2. Add rest of ingredients, except ½ cup peas.
3. Simmer gently for 30–45 minutes, or until vegetables are cooked but not mushy.
4. Take pan off heat and stir in peas. Allow soup to stand for 1 hour before serving.
5. Reheat just until heated through and serve.

Lentil Vegetable Soup

Mary C. Jungerman, Boulder, CO

Makes 10 servings (about ⅔ cup per serving)

Prep. Time: 15 minutes   *Cooking Time: 2 hours*

- 2 cups lentils
- 8 cups water
- 2 slices bacon, diced
- ½ cup chopped onion
- ½ cup chopped celery
- ¼ cup chopped carrots
- 3 Tbsp. snipped fresh parsley
- 1 clove garlic, minced
- 2 tsp. salt
- ¼ tsp. pepper
- ½ tsp. dry oregano
- 2 cups chopped tomatoes
- 2 Tbsp. wine vinegar

1. Rinse lentils. Drain and place in large soup kettle. Add water and all remaining ingredients except tomatoes and vinegar.
2. Cover and simmer 1½ hours.
3. Add tomatoes and vinegar. Cover and simmer for 30 minutes longer.
4. Adjust seasoning and serve.

Veggie Minestrone

Dorothy VanDeest, Memphis, TN

Makes 8 servings

Prep. Time: 5 minutes *Cooking Time: 4 minutes*

2 Tbsp. olive oil
1 large onion, chopped
1 clove garlic, minced
4 cups low-sodium chicken or vegetable stock
16-oz. can kidney beans, rinsed and drained
14½-oz. can no-salt-added diced tomatoes
2 medium carrots, sliced thin
¼ tsp. dry oregano
¼ tsp. pepper
½ cup dry whole wheat elbow macaroni
4 oz. fresh spinach
½ cup grated Parmesan cheese

1. Set the Instant Pot to the Sauté function and heat the olive oil.

2. When the olive oil is heated, add the onion and garlic to the inner pot and sauté for 5 minutes.

3. Press Cancel and add the stock, kidney beans, tomatoes, carrots, oregano, and pepper. Gently pour in the macaroni, but do not stir. Just push the noodles gently under the liquid.

4. Secure the lid and set the vent to sealing.

5. Manually set the cook time for 4 minutes on high pressure.

6. When the cooking time is over, manually release the pressure and remove the lid when the pin drops.

7. Stir in the spinach and let wilt a few minutes.

8. Sprinkle 1 Tbsp. grated Parmesan on each individual bowl of soup. Enjoy!

Cannellini Bean Soup

Hope Comerford, Clinton Township, MI

Makes 6–8 servings

Prep. Time: 10 minutes · *Soaking Time: overnight* · *Cooking Time: 30 minutes*

2 Tbsp. extra-virgin olive oil
4 cloves garlic, sliced very thin
1 small onion, chopped
2 heads escarole, well washed and cut medium-fine (about 8 cups)
8-oz. bag dry cannellini beans, soaked overnight
8 cups low-sodium chicken stock
3 basil leaves, chopped fine
Parmesan cheese shavings, *optional*

1. Set the Instant Pot to Sauté and heat the olive oil.
2. Sauté the garlic, onion, and escarole until the onion is translucent.
3. Hit the Cancel button on your Instant Pot and add the beans and chicken stock.
4. Secure the lid and set the vent to sealing.
5. Manually set the time for 25 minutes on high pressure.
6. When the cooking time is over, let the pressure release naturally. Remove the lid when the pin drops and spoon into serving bowls.
7. Top each bowl with a sprinkle of the chopped basil leaves and a few Parmesan shavings (if using).

Tip:

If you do not remember to soak the beans overnight, or if you don't have time to soak them, simply cook the soup on high pressure for 51 minutes instead.

French Onion Soup

Hope Comerford, Clinton Township, MI

Makes 6–8 servings

Prep. Time: 10 minutes ⁂ *Cooking Time: 7–8 hours* ⁂ *Ideal slow-cooker size: 5-qt.*

- 3–4 large sweet yellow onions, sliced thinly
- ½ tsp. pepper
- 1 bay leaf
- 2 sprigs fresh thyme
- 7 cups low-sodium beef stock
- 1 cup dry white wine (such as a chardonnay)
- 6–8 slices bread, crusts removed
- 4 oz. Gruyère cheese, sliced thinly

1. Place the onions into the crock and sprinkle them with the pepper. Add the bay leaf and sprigs of thyme.
2. Pour in the beef stock and wine.
3. Cover and cook on Low for 7–8 hours. Remove the thyme sprigs and bay leaf.
4. Serve each serving of soup in an oven-safe bowl and cover the soup with a slice of bread topped with cheese. Place it in the oven under the broiler for a few minutes, or until the cheese starts to bubble.

Wild-Rice Mushroom Soup

Kelly Amos, Pittsboro, NC

Makes 4 servings

Prep. Time: 15–20 minutes · *Cooking Time: 35 minutes*

- 1 Tbsp. olive oil
- ½ white onion, chopped
- ¼ cup chopped celery
- ¼ cup chopped carrots
- 1½ cups sliced fresh white mushrooms
- ½ cup white wine, or ½ cup low-sodium, fat-free chicken broth
- 2½ cups low-sodium, fat-free chicken broth
- 1 cup fat-free half-and-half
- 2 Tbsp. flour
- ¼ tsp. dry thyme
- Black pepper to taste
- 1 cup cooked wild rice

1. Put olive oil in stockpot and heat. Carefully add chopped onion, celery, and carrots. Cook until tender.
2. Add mushrooms, white wine, and chicken broth.
3. Cover and heat through.
4. In a bowl, blend half-and-half, flour, thyme, and pepper. Then stir in cooked wild rice.
5. Pour rice mixture into hot stockpot with vegetables.
6. Cook over medium heat. Stir continually until thickened and bubbly.

Easy Cream of Vegetable Soup

Norma Grieser, Sebring, FL

Makes 6 cups

Prep. Time: 20 minutes ❧ *Cooking Time: 20 minutes*

¼ cup chopped celery
¼ cup chopped onion
1 Tbsp. canola oil
3 Tbsp. flour
½ tsp. salt
Pepper to taste
1 bay leaf, or herb of your choice
3 cups skim milk
2 cups fresh or frozen vegetables of your choice, cut up or sliced (spinach, asparagus, broccoli, cauliflower, peas, carrots, tomatoes, mushrooms); if using canned vegetables, use ones without added salt

1. In large stockpot, sauté celery and onion in oil.
2. Over low heat, stir in flour, salt, pepper, and herb.
3. Add milk, stirring constantly. Cook over medium heat until hot and bubbly.
4. Steam or microwave vegetables until crisp-tender.
5. Remove bay leaf, if using. Stir vegetables into thickened creamy sauce and heat through.

Tips:

1. If you want cream of chicken soup, add reduced-sodium chicken bouillon.
2. This recipe can be used as soup itself, or you can use it in any recipe calling for cream soup.

Creamy Tomato Soup

Susie Shenk Wenger, Lancaster, PA

Makes 4 servings

Prep. Time: 10–15 minutes · *Cooking Time: 3–4 hours* · *Ideal slow-cooker size: 3-qt.*

- 29-oz. can tomato sauce, or crushed tomatoes, or 1 qt. home-canned tomatoes, chopped
- 1 small onion, chopped
- 1–2 carrots, sliced thin
- 2 tsp. brown sugar
- 1 tsp. Italian seasoning
- ¼ tsp. salt
- ¼ tsp. pepper
- 1 tsp. freshly chopped parsley
- ½ tsp. Worcestershire sauce
- 1 cup heaving whipping cream
- Croutons, preferably homemade
- Freshly grated Parmesan cheese

1. Combine tomato sauce, onion, carrots, brown sugar, Italian seasoning, salt, pepper, parsley, and Worcestershire sauce in slow cooker.
2. Cover. Cook on Low 3–4 hours, or until vegetables are soft.
3. Cool soup a bit. Puree with immersion blender.
4. Add cream and blend lightly again.
5. Serve hot with croutons and Parmesan as garnish.

Tip:

This recipe can be easily doubled.

Creamy Broccoli Soup

SuAnne Burkholder, Millersburg, OH

Makes 3–4 servings

Prep. Time: 10–15 minutes ♣ *Cooking Time: 15–20 minutes*

4 cups milk, *divided*
1 Tbsp. chicken-flavored soup base
1½ cups cut-up broccoli
2 Tbsp. cornstarch
Salt to taste

1. Heat 3 cups milk and chicken base in a stockpot over low heat until hot.

2. Meanwhile, place cut-up broccoli in a microwave-safe dish. Add 1 Tbsp. water. Cover. Microwave on High for 1½ minutes. Stir. Repeat until broccoli becomes bright green and just-tender. Be careful not to overcook it! Drain liquid from broccoli.

3. In a small bowl, or in a jar with a tight-fitting lid, mix 1 cup milk and cornstarch until smooth. Slowly add to hot milk mixture.

4. Simmer gently, stirring constantly. When slightly thickened, add broccoli and salt.

Garden Chili

Stacy Schmucker Stoltzfus, Enola, PA

Makes 10 servings

Prep. Time: 45 minutes · *Cooking Time: 6–8 hours* · *Ideal slow-cooker size: 3½- or 4-qt.*

- ¾ lb. onions, chopped
- 1 tsp. minced garlic
- 1 Tbsp. olive oil
- ¾ cup chopped celery
- 1 large carrot, peeled and thinly sliced
- 1 large green bell pepper, chopped
- 1 small zucchini, sliced
- ¼ lb. fresh mushrooms, sliced
- 1¼ cups water
- 14-oz. can kidney beans, rinsed and drained
- 14-oz. can low-sodium diced tomatoes with juice
- 1 tsp. lemon juice
- ⅛ tsp. dry oregano
- 1 tsp. ground cumin
- 1 tsp. chili powder
- 1 tsp. salt
- 1 tsp. black pepper

1. Sauté onions and garlic in olive oil in large skillet over medium heat until tender.
2. Add remaining fresh veggies. Sauté 2–3 minutes. Transfer to slow cooker.
3. Add remaining ingredients.
4. Cover. Cook on Low 6–8 hours.

Serving suggestion:

This is good served over rice.

Three Bean Chili

Deb Kepiro, Strasburg, PA

Makes 6 servings

Prep. Time: 15 minutes · *Cooking Time: 30–60 minutes*

- 1 large onion, chopped
- 2 Tbsp. oil
- 15½-oz. can kidney beans, rinsed and drained
- 15½-oz. can pinto beans, rinsed and drained
- 15½-oz. can black beans, rinsed and drained
- 2 (14½-oz.) cans diced tomatoes
- 1 cup vegetable broth
- ¾ cup salsa
- 1 tsp. cumin
- ¼ tsp. salt
- Shredded cheese, *optional*
- Green onions, *optional*
- Sour cream, *optional*

1. In a soup pot, sauté onion in oil until tender.
2. Add beans, tomatoes, broth, salsa, cumin, and salt.
3. Bring to a boil. Cover. Reduce heat and let simmer for 30–60 minutes.
4. If desired, garnish with shredded cheese, green onions, and sour cream.

Variation:

Add 1 cup corn, 1 Tbsp. chili powder, and 15½-oz. can undrained chili beans.

—Moreen Weaver, Bath, NY

Main Dishes

Chicken & Turkey

Chicken Baked with Red Onions, Potatoes, and Rosemary

OVEN

Kristine Stalter, Iowa City, IA

Makes 8 servings

Prep. Time: 10–15 minutes ✤ *Baking Time: 45–60 minutes*

- 2 red onions, each cut into 10 wedges
- 1¼ lb. new potatoes, unpeeled and cut into chunks
- 2 garlic bulbs, separated into cloves, unpeeled
- Salt and pepper to taste
- 3 tsp. extra-virgin olive oil
- 2 Tbsp. balsamic vinegar
- Approximately 5 sprigs rosemary
- 8 chicken thighs, skin removed

1. Spread onions, potatoes, and garlic in single layer over bottom of large roasting pan so that they will crisp and brown.
2. Season with salt and pepper.
3. Pour over the oil and balsamic vinegar and add rosemary, leaving some sprigs whole and stripping the leaves off the rest.
4. Toss vegetables and seasonings together.
5. Tuck chicken pieces among vegetables.
6. Bake at 400°F for 45–60 minutes, or until chicken and vegetables are cooked through.
7. Transfer to a big platter, or take to the table in the roasting pan.

Lemon-Chicken Oven Bake

Judi Manos, West Islip, NY

Makes 4 servings

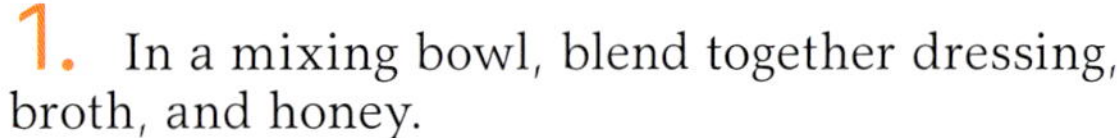

¼ cup zesty Italian dressing
½ cup chicken broth
1 Tbsp. honey
1½ lb. bone-in chicken legs and thighs
1 lb. new potatoes, quartered
5 cloves garlic, peeled
1 lemon, cut in 8 wedges
1 tsp. dry rosemary, *optional*

1. In a mixing bowl, blend together dressing, broth, and honey.
2. Arrange chicken, potatoes, and garlic in well-greased 9 × 13-inch baking dish.
3. Drizzle with dressing mixture.
4. Situate lemons and rosemary, if using, among the chicken and potatoes.
5. Bake at 400°F for 45–50 minutes, or until chicken is done and potatoes are tender. (Temperature probe inserted into center of chicken should register 165°F.)
6. Serve lemons as garnish if you wish.

Chicken Parmesan

Jessalyn Wantland, Napoleon, OH

Makes 4 servings

Prep. Time: 10 minutes *Baking Time: 45 minutes*

4 boneless, skinless chicken breast halves, about 6 oz. each
1 egg, beaten
¾ cup Italian-seasoned breadcrumbs
25-oz. jar pasta sauce
1 cup shredded Parmesan cheese

1. Grease a 7 × 11-inch baking dish.
2. Place egg in a shallow bowl.
3. Place breadcrumbs in another shallow bowl.
4. Dip each piece of chicken in egg, and then in breadcrumbs.
5. Place coated chicken in baking dish.
6. Bake at 400°F for 30 minutes.
7. Spoon pasta sauce over chicken.
8. Top evenly with cheese.
9. Bake another 15 minutes, or until heated through and cheese is melted.

Butter Chicken

Jessica Stoner, Arlington, OH

Makes 4 servings

Prep. Time: 10–15 minutes *Cooking Time: 20 minutes*

- 1 Tbsp. olive oil
- 1 medium onion, diced
- 1–2 medium cloves garlic, minced
- ½ Tbsp. minced ginger
- 1 tsp. garam masala
- ½ tsp. turmeric
- 2 tsp. kosher salt
- 2 lb. cubed boneless, skinless chicken breasts
- ¼ cup tomato paste
- 2 cups crushed tomatoes
- 1½ cups water
- ½ Tbsp. honey
- 1½ cups heavy cream
- 1 Tbsp. butter

1. On Sauté function at high heat, heat the oil in the inner pot of the Instant Pot. Add the onion, garlic, and ginger and sauté for 1 minute, until fragrant and onion is soft.

2. Add the garam masala, turmeric, and salt. Sauté quickly and add the chicken. Stir to coat chicken. Add the tomato paste and crushed tomatoes. Slowly add the water, scraping the bottom of the pot with a spoon to make sure there are no bits of tomato stuck to the bottom. Stir in the honey.

3. Secure the lid, making sure vent is turned to sealing function. Use the Poultry high pressure function and set cook time to 15 minutes. Once done cooking, do a quick release of the pressure.

4. Remove lid and change to medium/normal Sauté function and stir in the heavy cream and bring to a simmer. Simmer for 5 minutes, adding up to ¼ cup additional water if you need to thin the sauce out. Stir in the butter until melted and turn off.

Serving suggestion:

Serve hot with basmati rice and naan.

Easy Chicken Fajitas

Jessica Hontz, Coatesville, PA

Makes 4–6 servings

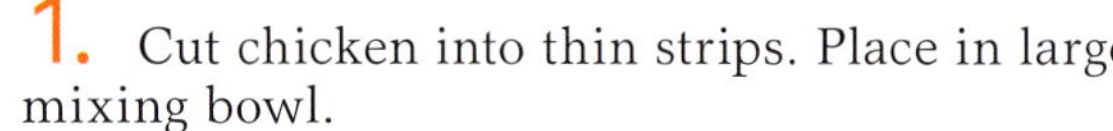

1 lb. boneless, skinless chicken breasts
1 pkg. dry Italian salad dressing mix
8-oz. bottle Italian salad dressing
1 cup salsa
1 green pepper, sliced
½ medium-sized onion, sliced
10 (10-inch) flour tortillas

Optional toppings:

Shredded Monterey Jack cheese
Shredded lettuce
Sour cream
Chopped tomatoes
Salsa
Hot pepper sauce

1. Cut chicken into thin strips. Place in large mixing bowl.

2. Add dry salad dressing mix and salad dressing. Mix well. Cover and marinade 4–8 hours in the fridge.

3. In a large skillet, combine drained chicken strips, salsa, and pepper and onion slices. Stir-fry until chicken is cooked and pepper and onion are soft.

4. Place chicken mix in tortillas with your choice of toppings.

Variation:

The cooked chicken can also be used on salads.

Garlic Mushroom Chicken Thighs

Elaine Vigoda, Rochester, NY

Makes 6 servings

Prep. Time: 15 minutes ✿ *Cooking Time: 4 hours* ✿ *Ideal slow-cooker size: 5-qt.*

- 6 boneless, skinless chicken thighs
- 3 Tbsp. flour
- 8–10 cloves garlic, peeled and very lightly crushed
- 1 Tbsp. oil
- ¾ lb. fresh mushrooms, any combination of varieties, cut into bite-sized pieces or slices
- ⅓ cup balsamic vinegar
- 1¼ cups chicken broth
- 1–2 bay leaves
- ½ tsp. dry thyme or 4 sprigs fresh thyme
- 2 tsp. apricot jam

1. Grease interior of slow-cooker crock.
2. Place flour in strong plastic bag without any holes. One by one, put each thigh in bag, hold the bag shut, and shake it to flour the thigh fully.
3. Place thighs in crock. If you need to make a second layer, stagger the pieces so they don't directly overlap.
4. If you have time, sauté garlic in oil in skillet just until it begins to brown.
5. Sprinkle garlic over thighs, including those on the bottom layer.
6. Scatter cut-up mushrooms over thighs, too, remembering those on the bottom layer.
7. Mix remaining ingredients together in a bowl, stirring to break up the jam.
8. When well mixed, pour into the cooker along the edges so you don't wash the vegetables off the chicken pieces.
9. Cover. Cook on Low for 4 hours, or until an instant-read meat thermometer registers 160°–165°F when stuck into the thighs.
10. Serve meat, topped with vegetables, with sauce spooned over.

Coq Au Vin

Bernadette Veenstra, Grand Rapids, MI

Makes 8 servings

Prep. Time: 35 minutes · *Cooking Time: 4–6 hours* · *Ideal slow-cooker size: oval 6 qt.*

3 slices bacon, cut into ¾-inch-wide pieces
8–10 oz. fresh mushrooms, cut in half
10-oz. pkg. frozen pearl onions
10 chicken thighs, skin removed
½ tsp. salt
¼ tsp. pepper
1 medium onion, chopped
1 large carrot, peeled and chopped
4 cloves garlic, chopped
1 cup dry red wine
2 Tbsp. tomato paste
1 bay leaf
¾ cup chicken broth

1. Grease interior of slow-cooker crock.
2. In a big nonstick skillet, cook bacon over medium heat until browned. Or place bacon pieces on a paper plate. Cover with a paper towel and microwave on High for 3 minutes.
3. Using a slotted spoon, transfer browned bacon to crock.
4. Gently stir mushroom pieces and pearl onions into bacon in crock.
5. Salt and pepper chicken thighs. Place on top of the vegetables in the crock. If you need to make two layers or more, stagger pieces so they don't directly overlap each other.
6. In a good-sized bowl, stir together onion, carrot, garlic, wine, tomato paste, bay leaf, and chicken broth, mixing well.
7. Spoon onion-carrot mixture over chicken pieces, lifting up thighs on top layer to add veggie mixture to tops of thighs underneath.
8. Cook for 4–6 hours on Low, or until instant-read meat thermometer registers 165°F when stuck in center of thighs (but not touching a bone).
9. To serve, discard bay leaf. Serve chicken, vegetables, and sauce in shallow bowls.

Serving suggestions:
This goes well with salad, crusty French bread, and couscous.

Skinny Chicken Stroganoff

Carol Sherwood, Batavia, NY

Makes 6 servings

Prep. Time: 10–15 minutes ✤ *Cooking Time: 20–25 minutes*

- 4 slices turkey bacon, cooked and broken
- 6 oz. dry whole wheat noodles
- ¾ cup reduced-fat sour cream
- ¼ cup all-purpose flour
- 14½-oz. can low-fat, low-sodium chicken broth
- ⅛ tsp. black pepper
- 1 lb. boneless, skinless chicken breasts, cut into ¼-inch strips
- 8 oz. sliced fresh mushrooms
- 1 cup chopped onion
- 1 clove garlic, pressed
- 2 Tbsp. snipped fresh parsley

1. Cook bacon until crisp in a large skillet. Remove from pan, break, and set aside.
2. Cook noodles according to package instructions. Drain and keep warm.
3. Meanwhile, in a good-sized bowl, whisk together sour cream and flour until smooth.
4. Gradually whisk in chicken broth until smooth. Stir in pepper. Set aside.
5. Heat skillet that you used for bacon over high heat until hot. Add chicken. Cook, stirring continually for 3 minutes, or until meat is no longer pink. Remove from pan and set aside. Keep warm.
6. Reduce heat to medium. Add mushrooms, onion, and garlic. Cook and stir 3 minutes.
7. Stir in chicken and bacon.
8. Stir in sour cream mixture. Bring to a boil.
9. Reduce heat. Simmer 2 minutes, stirring constantly.
10. Remove from heat. Stir in parsley.
11. Serve over prepared noodles.

Chicken in Alfredo Sauce

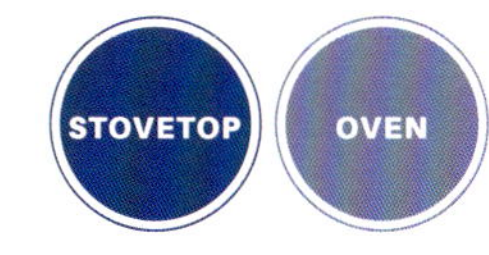

Joyce Clark, East Amherst, NY

Makes 4–6 servings

Prep. Time: 20–30 minutes ❧ *Cooking/Baking Time: 30–35 minutes*

½ cup cooked spinach, stems removed, or frozen chopped spinach, thawed

4 boneless, skinless chicken breast halves, slightly flattened

2 thin slices ham, each cut in half

¼ red bell pepper, cut in thin strips

1 Tbsp. butter

2 Tbsp. flour

1 clove garlic, minced

¾ cup whipping cream

1¼ cups milk

1 tsp. lemon zest

Pinch ground nutmeg

¼ tsp. salt

¼ cup grated Parmesan cheese

1 Tbsp. chopped fresh parsley

Cooked rice or pasta

1. Squeeze spinach until dry. Divide evenly over chicken breasts. Top each breast with a half slice of ham and a few red pepper strips.

2. Roll breasts up firmly, beginning at thinnest end of breast. Secure each with a toothpick and place, seam side down, in a single layer in a greased baking pan. Set aside.

3. In a small saucepan, melt butter. Add flour, garlic, cream, milk, lemon zest, nutmeg, salt, Parmesan cheese, and parsley. Stir and blend well. Cook over low heat, stirring occasionally until sauce begins to gently boil. Then stir continuously until smooth and thickened. Pour over chicken rolls.

4. Cover and bake at 350°F for 20 minutes, turning after 10 minutes. Baste rolls with sauce.

5. Uncover and stir sauce as well as you can. Spoon up over chicken. Bake 5–7 minutes more.

6. To serve, cut meat rolls in half and serve over rice or pasta. Whisk sauce smooth and ladle over top.

Mexi Chicken Rotini

Jane Geigley, Lancaster, PA

Makes 6 servings

Prep. Time: 30 minutes ♣ *Cooking Time: 4½ hours* ♣ *Ideal slow-cooker size: 4-qt.*

1 cup water
3 cups partially cooked rotini
12-oz. pkg. frozen mixed vegetables
10-oz. can Ro*Tel diced tomatoes with green chilies
4-oz. can green chilies, undrained
4 cups shredded cooked chicken
1 cup low-fat shredded cheddar cheese

1. Combine all ingredients in slow cooker except shredded cheddar.

2. Cover and cook on Low for 4 hours.

3. Top with shredded cheddar, then let cook covered an additional 20 minutes or so, or until cheese is melted.

Now That's Lasagna

Shirley Unternahrer, Wayland, IA

Makes 10 servings

Prep. Time: 20 minutes *Cooking Time: 4 hours* *Ideal slow-cooker size: 6-qt.*

1 lb. ground turkey sausage

1 small onion, chopped

1 small bell pepper, chopped

1 qt. low-sodium tomato juice, *divided*

15 dry gluten-free lasagna noodles, *divided*

12 oz. low-fat cottage cheese, *divided*

3 cups shredded low-fat mozzarella cheese, *divided*

28-oz. jar organic no-sugar-added spaghetti sauce of your choice, *divided*

6 oz. sliced turkey pepperoni

1. Brown sausage in skillet. Drain off the drippings. Add chopped onion and pepper to skillet. Sauté 3 minutes with meat.

2. Pour 1 cup tomato juice into slow cooker as first layer.

3. Add a layer of 5 uncooked lasagna noodles. Break to fit inside curved edges of slow cooker.

4. Spread with half of cottage cheese as next layer. Spoon half of meat/veggie mix over cottage cheese. Sprinkle with 1 cup mozzarella cheese. Spoon half of spaghetti sauce over grated cheese.

5. Add another layer of 5 lasagna noodles.

6. Add remaining cottage cheese, followed by a layer of remaining meat/veggie mix. Add remaining 5 noodles.

7. Top with pepperoni slices, remaining spaghetti sauce, and half of remaining mozzarella cheese. Pour rest of tomato juice slowly around edge of cooker and its ingredients.

8. Cover. Cook on High 3½ hours. Remove lid and top with remaining mozzarella cheese. Cook another 15 minutes.

9. Allow lasagna to rest 15–20 minutes before serving.

Easy Chicken Enchiladas

Lois Peterson, Huron, SD

Makes 4 servings

Prep. Time: 35–45 minutes · *Baking Time: 40 minutes*

10¾-oz. can cream of chicken soup
½ cup sour cream
1 cup picante sauce
2 tsp. chili powder
2 cups chopped cooked chicken
1 cup grated pepper Jack cheese
6 (6-inch) flour tortillas
1 medium tomato, chopped
1 green onion, sliced

1. Stir soup, sour cream, picante sauce, and chili powder in a medium bowl.
2. In a large bowl, combine 1 cup sauce mixture, chicken, and cheese.
3. Grease 9 × 13-inch baking dish.
4. Divide mixture among tortillas.
5. Roll up each tortilla. Place in baking dish, seam side down.
6. Pour remaining sauce mixture over filled tortillas.
7. Cover. Bake at 350°F for 40 minutes or until enchiladas are hot and bubbling.
8. Top with chopped tomato and onion and serve.

Chicken and Broccoli Bake

Jan Rankin, Millersville, PA

Makes 12–16 servings

Prep. Time: 15 minutes ♦ *Baking Time: 30 minutes*

- 2 (10¾-oz.) cans cream of chicken soup
- 2½ cups milk, *divided*
- 16-oz. bag frozen chopped broccoli, thawed and drained
- 3 cups cooked, chopped chicken breast
- 2 cups buttermilk baking mix

1. Mix soup and 1 cup milk together in large mixing bowl until smooth.
2. Stir in broccoli and chicken.
3. Pour into well-greased 9 × 13-inch baking dish.
4. Mix together 1½ cups milk and baking mix in mixing bowl.
5. Spoon evenly over top of chicken/broccoli mixture.
6. Bake at 450°F for 30 minutes.

Chicken and Dumplings

Barbara Nolan, Pleasant Valley, NY

Makes 4 servings

Prep. Time: 15 minutes ❧ *Cooking Time: 30 minutes*

4 carrots, cut into ½-inch-thick slices
2 medium onions, cut into eighths
1 clove garlic, sliced thin
3 celery ribs, cut into ½-inch-thick slices
2 Tbsp. butter
3 Tbsp. flour
2 (14-oz.) cans chicken broth
1 lb. uncooked chicken cutlets, cut into 1-inch cubes
2 Tbsp. grated carrots
½ tsp. poultry seasoning
¼ tsp. garlic powder
⅛ tsp. black pepper
¼ cup half-and-half
Fresh parsley

Dumplings:

1½ cups flour
2 tsp. baking powder
¾ tsp. salt
1 cup milk
1 egg
2 Tbsp. vegetable oil

1. Sauté carrot pieces, onions, garlic, and celery in butter in medium saucepan for 3 minutes, or until vegetables soften.
2. Sprinkle with flour.
3. Stir to combine. Cook 1–2 minutes.
4. Stir in chicken broth, chicken, grated carrots, poultry seasoning, garlic powder, and pepper until smooth.
5. Bring to boil. Simmer 5 minutes, or until thickened, stirring constantly.
6. To prepare dumplings, mix the flour, baking powder, and salt in mixing bowl.
7. In a separate bowl, combine milk, egg, and oil.
8. Add egg-milk mixture to dry ingredients, barely mixing.
9. Drop dumpling batter by tablespoonfuls onto simmering chicken.
10. Cook 10 minutes uncovered.
11. Cover and cook an additional 10 minutes.
12. Pour half-and-half between dumplings. into broth.
13. Scatter fresh parsley over top. Serve immediately.

Tip:

Speed up your prep by chopping chicken and veggies and refrigerating until ready.

Crustless Chicken Pot Pie

Hope Comerford, Clinton Township, MI

Makes 6 servings

Prep Time: 15 minutes ✿ Cook Time: 30 minutes

- 1 lb. boneless, skinless chicken breasts
- 3 Yukon Gold potatoes, peeled and chopped into ½-inch cubes
- 1 cup chopped onion
- 2 carrots, chopped
- ¾ cup frozen peas
- ¾ cup frozen corn
- ½ cup chopped celery
- 10¾-oz. can condensed cream of chicken soup
- 1 cup milk
- 1 cup chicken broth
- 1 tsp. salt
- 1 tsp. garlic powder
- 1 tsp. onion powder
- 16.3-oz. can flaky biscuits
- 2 Tbsp. cornstarch
- 2 Tbsp. cold water

1. Place all ingredients, except for the biscuits, cornstarch, and water, into the inner pot of the Instant Pot.

2. Secure the lid and set the vent to sealing. Manually set the cook time for 25 minutes on high pressure.

3. While the Instant Pot is cooking, bake the canned biscuits according to the directions on the can.

4. When the cook time is over, manually release the pressure.

5. When the pin drops, remove the lid. Remove the chicken to a bowl. Press Cancel then press Sauté.

6. Mix together the cornstarch and water. Stir this into the contents of the Instant Pot and cook until thickened, about 5 minutes. Meanwhile, shred the chicken, then add it back in with the contents of the inner pot.

7. Serve with the freshly baked flaky biscuits.

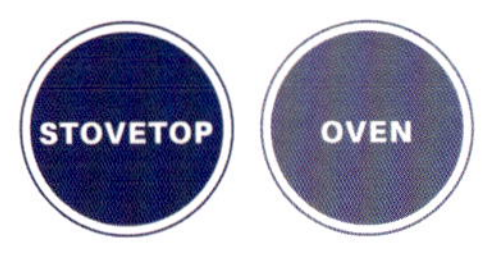

Country Gal's Chicken Pot Pie

MarJanita Martin, Batesburg, SC

Makes 4–6 servings

Prep. Time: 30 minutes · *Baking Time: 45 minutes*

2 refrigerated pie crusts
2 Tbsp. butter
12½-oz. canned chicken, drained
1 tsp. seasoned salt
½ tsp. pepper
2½ cups frozen mixed vegetables
1 cup shredded cheese
1 egg, beaten
1 Tbsp. water

Sauce:

3 Tbsp. butter
1 medium onion, sliced
⅓ cup flour
½ tsp. salt
½ tsp. pepper
1 Tbsp. Italian seasoning
1 sprig rosemary, chopped
2 basil leaves, chopped
1¾ cups chicken stock
⅔ cups half-and-half

1. Put one crust in the pie dish. Prick the bottom crust with a fork.
2. Melt the 2 Tbsp. of butter in a large saucepan.
3. Add chicken, seasoned salt, and pepper.
4. Add in veggies and cook until almost tender.
5. Remove from saucepan and set aside.
6. Make the sauce: Use the saucepan and melt the 3 Tbsp. of butter.
7. Add the onion and cook until translucent.
8. Whisk in flour, salt, pepper, Italian seasoning, rosemary, and basil.
9. Pour in chicken stock and half-and-half, stirring constantly. Simmer until thickened.
10. Add veggies and chicken into the sauce. Gently stir. Pour this mixture into pie dish.
11. Add the shredded cheese over top, then place other crust over top.
12. Seal and crimp edges, while cutting away any excess dough. Slit the crust.
13. Whisk together egg and water. Brush over the top of the pie.
14. Bake at 350°F for 45 minutes.
15. Remove and let stand 10 minutes before serving.

Glazed Barbecue Turkey Meatloaf

Hope Comerford, Clinton Township, MI

Makes 6–8 servings

Prep. Time: 15–20 minutes ✤ *Cooking Time: 4–5 hours* ✤ *Ideal slow-cooker size: 5-qt. oval*

2 lb. ground turkey
1 large egg
1¼ cups gluten-free or regular panko breadcrumbs
1 Tbsp. garlic powder
1 Tbsp. onion powder
3 tsp. dry minced onion
1 tsp. Italian seasoning
6 dashes Worcestershire sauce
¼ cup barbecue sauce

Glaze:

3 Tbsp. brown sugar
¼ cup barbecue sauce
1 tsp. dry mustard

1. Spray crock with nonstick spray.
2. Make a tinfoil sling for your slow cooker so you can lift the cooked meatloaf out easily. Begin by folding a strip of foil accordion-fashion so that it's about 1½–2 inches wide, and long enough to fit from the top edge of the crock, down inside and up the other side, plus a 2-inch overhang on each side of the cooker. Make a second strip exactly like the first.
3. Place the one strip in the crock, running from end to end. Place the second strip in the crock, running from side to side. The 2 strips should form a cross in the bottom of the crock.
4. In a bowl, mix all of the meatloaf ingredients, then shape it into a loaf. Place it in the crock, centering it where the foil handles cross.
5. Cover and cook on Low 4–5 hours.
6. Remove the meatloaf from the crock using the handles and place on a baking sheet.
7. Mix the glaze ingredients together. Spoon this over the top of the meatloaf.
8. Place the meatloaf in the oven under the broiler for 2–4 minutes, so that the glaze thickens and browns, but be careful not to let it burn.
9. Let it stand for 10 minutes, then slice and serve.

Barbecue Chicken Pizza

OVEN STOVETOP

Hope Comerford, Clinton Township, MI

Makes 6 servings

Prep. Time: 10 minutes ❧ *Cooking/Baking Time: 13–15 minutes*

14 oz. premade or homemade pizza dough

½ cup sliced red onion

1 Tbsp. olive oil

1½ cups diced rotisserie chicken meat

1½ cups of your favorite barbecue sauce, *divided*

3 cups mozzarella cheese

⅓ cup chopped fresh cilantro

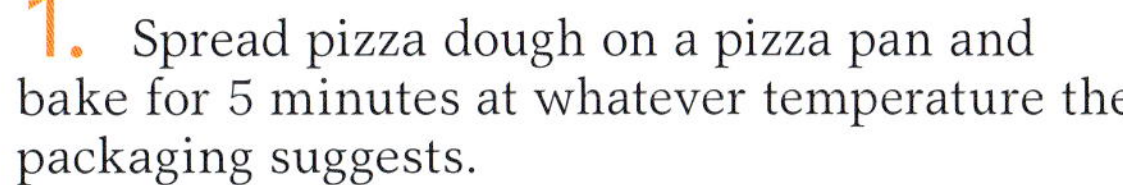

1. Spread pizza dough on a pizza pan and bake for 5 minutes at whatever temperature the packaging suggests.
2. While the pizza dough is cooking, sauté the red onion pieces in the olive oil until they are translucent. Set aside.
3. When the pizza crust has finished its 5 minutes, remove it.
4. Spread ½ cup of the barbecue sauce over the pizza crust.
5. Toss the rotisserie chicken meat with the remaining barbecue sauce and arrange it on the pizza crust.
6. Arrange the sautéed red onion pieces on the pizza crust.
7. Sprinkle the mozzarella cheese evenly over the toppings on the pizza.

8. Bake the pizza for 8–10 minutes, or until the cheese is melted and crust is golden brown.
9. When you remove the pizza, sprinkle it with the cilantro.
10. Serve and enjoy!

Pork

Pork Chops with Apple Stuffing

Arlene Yoder, Hartville, OH

Makes 6 servings

Prep. Time: 20 minutes ❧ *Cooking Time: 45–60 minutes*

- 6 bone-in pork chops, at least 1-inch thick, about 2 lb. total
- 1 Tbsp. canola oil
- ¼ cup chopped celery
- ¼ cup chopped onion
- 3 apples, peeled, cored, and diced
- ¼ cup sugar
- ½ cup breadcrumbs, or cracker crumbs
- ¼ tsp. salt
- ¼ tsp. pepper
- 2 tsp. chopped parsley

1. Cut a pocket about 1½-inch deep into the side of each chop for stuffing.
2. Heat oil in skillet.
3. Stir celery and onion into oil in skillet. Cook over medium heat until tender, stirring frequently.
4. Stir in diced apples. Sprinkle with sugar.
5. Cover skillet. Cook apples over low heat until tender and glazed.
6. Stir in breadcrumbs.
7. Stir in salt, pepper, and parsley.
8. Spreading open the pocket in each chop with your fingers, stuff with mixture.
9. Return half of stuffed chops to skillet. Brown on both sides over medium to high heat.
10. Remove browned chops to platter. Cover to keep warm.
11. Repeat Step 9 with remaining chops.
12. Return other chops to skillet.
13. Reduce heat. Add a few tablespoons of water.
14. Cover. Cook slowly over low heat until done, about 20–25 minutes.

Paprika Pork Chops with Rice

Sharon Easter, Yuba City, CA

Makes 4 servings

Prep. Time: 5 minutes & *Cooking Time: 30 minutes*

⅛ tsp. pepper
1 tsp. paprika
4–5 thick-cut boneless pork chops (1–1½ inches thick)
1 Tbsp. olive oil
1¼ cups water, *divided*
1 onion, sliced
½ green bell pepper, sliced in rings
1½ cups canned no-salt-added stewed tomatoes
1 cup brown rice

1. Mix the pepper and paprika in a flat dish. Dredge the chops in the seasoning mixture.
2. Set the Instant Pot to the Sauté function and heat the oil in the inner pot.
3. Brown the chops on both sides for 1 to 2 minutes a side. Remove the pork chops and set aside.
4. Pour a small amount of water into the inner pot and scrape up any bits from the bottom with a wooden spoon. Press Cancel.
5. Place the browned chops side by side in the inner pot. Place 1 slice onion and 1 ring of green pepper on top of each chop. Spoon tomatoes with their juices over the top.
6. Pour the rice in and pour the remaining water over the top.
7. Secure the lid and set the vent to sealing.
8. Manually set the cook time for 30 minutes on high pressure.
9. When the cooking time is over, manually release the pressure.

Pork Roast and Vegetables

Jenny R. Unternahrer, Wayland, IA

Makes 8–10 servings

Prep. Time: 15 minutes ✤ *Cooking Time: 6–8 hours* ✤ *Ideal slow-cooker size: 5–qt.*

- 3 Tbsp. olive oil
- 3–4-lb. boneless pork chuck roast, trimmed
- Salt and pepper to taste
- ¼ cup flour
- 2 Tbsp. tomato paste
- 1/[illegible] cup dry white wine
- 1½ cups low-sodium beef or chicken broth
- 1 Tbsp. Worcestershire sauce
- 1 medium onion, thinly sliced (more or less onion, as you like)
- Handful baby carrots
- 2 small stalks celery, thinly sliced
- 3 cloves garlic, diced
- ½ tsp. dry thyme
- Small potatoes, quartered

1. Heat oil in pan (preferably not a nonstick). Sprinkle roast with salt and pepper. Sear roast on all sides until browned, approximately 10 minutes. Place in slow cooker.

2. Add flour and tomato paste to pan and cook for 1 minute. Add wine, broth, and Worcestershire sauce, scraping the bits off the bottom of the pan.

3. Pour over roast. Mix vegetables, garlic, and dry thyme in bowl and add to crock.

4. Cover and cook for 6–8 hours on Low. Add quartered potatoes to liquid after 4 hours. Serve in bowl so you can ladle the gravy over the top.

Carnitas

Hope Comerford, Clinton Township, MI

Makes 12 servings

Prep. Time: 10 minutes ✤ *Cooking Time: 15 minutes*

- 2 lb. pork shoulder roast, cut into 1-inch chunks
- 1½ tsp. kosher salt
- ½ tsp. pepper
- 2 tsp. cumin
- 5 cloves garlic, minced
- 1 tsp. oregano
- 3 bay leaves
- 2 cups chicken stock
- 1 tsp. lime zest
- 2 Tbsp. lime juice
- 12 (6-inch) gluten-free white corn tortillas, warmed

1. Place all ingredients, except the lime zest, lime juice, and tortillas, into the inner pot of the Instant Pot.

2. Secure the lid and set the vent to sealing. Manually set the cook time for 15 minutes on high pressure.

3. When cook time is up, let the pressure release naturally.

4. Add the lime juice and lime zest to the Inner Pot and stir. You may choose to shred the pork if you wish. Remove the bay leaves.

5. Serve on the white corn tortillas.

Salsa Verde Pork

Hope Comerford, Clinton Township, MI

Makes 6 servings

Prep. Time: 20 minutes ∗ *Cooking Time: 6–6½ hours* ∗ *Ideal slow-cooker size: 4-qt.*

1½-lb. boneless pork loin
1 large sweet onion, halved and sliced
2 large tomatoes, chopped
16-oz. jar gluten-free salsa verde (green salsa)
½ cup dry white wine
4 cloves garlic, minced
1 tsp. cumin
½ tsp. chili powder

1. Place the pork loin in the crock and add the rest of the ingredients on top.

2. Cover and cook on Low for 6–6½ hours.

3. Break apart the pork with two forks and mix with contents of crock.

Serving suggestion:

Serve over cooked brown rice or quinoa.

Simple Shredded Pork Tacos

Jennifer Freed, Rockingham, AL

Makes 6 servings

Prep. Time: 5 minutes · *Cooking Time: 8 hours* · *Ideal slow-cooker size: 4-qt.*

2-lb. boneless pork roast
1 cup salsa
4-oz. can chopped green chilies
½ tsp. garlic salt
½ tsp. black pepper

1. Place all ingredients in slow cooker.
2. Cover; cook on Low 8 hours, or until meat is tender.
3. To serve, use 2 forks to shred pork.

Serving suggestion:
Serve with taco shells and your favorite taco fixings.

Sausage, Carrots, Potatoes, and Cabbage

Hope Comerford, Clinton Township, MI

Makes 4 servings

Prep. Time: 5 minutes · *Cooking Time: 10 minutes*

1 Tbsp. olive oil
4 Tbsp. butter
1 large onion, sliced
14-oz. pkg. smoked sausage, sliced
1 cup chicken broth
2 carrots, peeled and chopped
2 lb. red potatoes, chopped
1 small head of cabbage, chopped
1½ tsp. sea salt
1½ tsp. smoked paprika
1 tsp. onion powder
¼ tsp. pepper

1. Set the Instant Pot to the Sauté function and let it get hot. Pour in the oil and butter.

2. Sauté the onion and sausage for about 4 minutes.

3. Pour in the broth and deglaze the bottom of the inner pot, scraping up any stuck-on bits. Press Cancel.

4. Add the remaining ingredients in the order listed.

5. Secure the lid and set the vent to sealing. Manually set the cook time for 6 minutes on high pressure.

6. When cook time is up, manually release the pressure.

Smoked Sausage and Sauerkraut

Joan Terwilliger, Lebanon, PA

Makes 6–8 servings

Prep. Time: 20 minutes ❧ *Baking Time: 1¾–2 hours*

- 2 Tbsp. butter
- 3 apples, peeled, halved, sliced thickly
- 1 large sweet onion, halved, sliced thickly
- 4 Yukon Gold potatoes, peeled, cut in ½-inch cubes
- ½ cup light brown sugar, packed
- ½ cup Dijon mustard
- ½–1 lb. kielbasa, sliced ½-inch thick, depending on amount of meat you like
- 1 cup apple cider, or Riesling
- 2 lb. sauerkraut, rinsed and drained

1. Melt butter in large ovenproof Dutch oven over medium-high heat.
2. Sauté apples and onion 10 minutes in butter, stirring occasionally.
3. Add potatoes.
4. In small bowl, mix the sugar and mustard. Add to onion-potato mixture.
5. Place sausage slices on top of onion/potato mixture.
6. Pour in cider or wine.
7. Place sauerkraut on top of sausage.
8. Bake, covered, at 350°F for 1¾–2 hours, or until potatoes are tender.

Stromboli

Monica Leaman Kehr, Portland, MI

Makes 6 servings

Prep. Time: 20 minutes · *Rising Time: 30–40 minutes*
Baking Time: 20 minutes · *Standing Time: 10 minutes*

- 1 loaf frozen bread dough, thawed
- Italian seasoning
- 2 cups grated mozzarella cheese
- 3 oz. sliced pepperoni
- 4 oz. chipped cooked ham
- ½ cup sliced black olives
- ⅓ cup sliced mushrooms, *optional*
- 2 Tbsp. chopped onions, *optional*
- 2 Tbsp. chopped green or red bell pepper, *optional*

1. Thaw bread dough and roll to 10 × 15-inch rectangle on lightly floured surface.
2. Sprinkle dough with Italian seasoning. Cover entire rectangle with cheese, pepperoni, ham, black olives, and any of the other ingredients you want. Press toppings down gently into dough.
3. Starting with the long side of the rectangle, roll dough up into a log shape. Seal ends by pinching dough together.
4. Carefully lift onto a lightly greased baking sheet. Cover and allow to rise 30–40 minutes.
5. Bake on sheet for 20 minutes at 400°F, or until lightly browned.
6. Allow to stand for 10 minutes before slicing.

TIP:

Microwave pepperoni slices between paper towels before putting in stromboli to eliminate some calories.

Mostaccioli

Sally Holzem, Schofield, WI

Makes 8 servings

Prep. Time: 45 minutes ❧ *Baking Time: 30–45 minutes*

- ½ lb. bulk Italian sausage
- ½ cup chopped onion
- 16-oz. can tomato paste
- ½ cup water
- ½ tsp. oregano
- ¼ tsp. pepper
- 4-oz. can sliced mushrooms, drained
- 14½-oz. can diced tomatoes, undrained
- ¾ cup tomato juice
- 8-oz. pkg. dry mostaccioli noodles
- 1½ cups cottage cheese
- ½ tsp. marjoram
- 12 oz. shredded mozzarella cheese, *divided*
- ½ cup grated Parmesan cheese

1. Brown sausage and onion in saucepan, stirring often to break up clumps. When pink no longer remains, drain off drippings.
2. Stir in tomato paste, water, oregano, pepper, mushrooms, tomatoes, and tomato juice.
3. Cover. Simmer 30 minutes over medium heat.
4. Meanwhile, prepare noodles according to package directions. Drain well.
5. In mixing bowl, combine cottage cheese and marjoram.
6. In greased 7 × 13-inch baking pan, layer in half of noodles.
7. Top with half of meat sauce.
8. Sprinkle with half of mozzarella.
9. Spoon cottage cheese mixture over top and spread as well as you can.
10. Layer on remaining noodles.
11. Top with remaining meat sauce.
12. Sprinkle with remaining mozzarella cheese.
13. Sprinkle with Parmesan cheese.
14. Bake at 350°F for 30–45 minutes, or until bubbly, heated through, and lightly browned.

Beef

Hearty Pot Roast

Colleen Heatwole, Burton, MI

Makes 12 servings (about 1 cup per serving)

Prep Time: 30 minutes · Roasting Time: 2–2½ hours · Standing Time: 10 minutes

- 4-lb. beef roast, ideally rump roast
- 4 medium red potatoes, cut in thirds
- 3 medium carrots, quartered
- 2 ribs celery, chopped
- 2 medium onions, sliced
- ½ cup flour
- 6-oz. can tomato paste
- ¼ cup water
- 1 tsp. instant beef bouillon, or 1 beef bouillon cube
- ¼ tsp. pepper

1. Place roast in 9 × 13-inch baking pan or roaster.
2. Arrange vegetables around roast.
3. Combine flour, tomato paste, water, bouillon, and pepper in small bowl.
4. Pour over meat and vegetables.
5. Cover. Roast at 325°F for 2–2½ hours, or until meat thermometer registers 170°F.
6. Allow meat to stand for 10 minutes.
7. Slice and place on platter surrounded by vegetables.
8. Pour gravy over top. Place additional gravy in bowl and serve along with platter.

Variation:

You can make this in a large oven cooking bag. Combine flour, tomato paste, water, bouillon, and pepper in a bowl. Pour into cooking bag. Place in 9 × 13-inch baking pan. Add roast to bag in pan. Add vegetables around roast in bag. Close bag with its tie. Make six 1/2-inch slits on top of bag. Roast according to instructions in Step 5 and following.

Aunt Iris's Barbecue Brisket

Carolyn Spohn, Shawnee, KS

Makes 10 servings (2 oz. meat with a little sauce)

Prep. Time: 20–30 minutes · Marinating Time: 8 hours, or overnight
Baking Time: 3–4 hours · Standing Time: 30 minutes

2-lb. lean beef brisket
¼ tsp. garlic powder
¼ tsp. onion powder
¼ tsp. celery salt
2 oz. liquid smoke
2 tsp. Worcestershire sauce

Barbecue sauce:
⅓ cup honey
¼ cup light soy sauce
⅔ cup ketchup
½ tsp. Tabasco sauce
1 tsp. dry mustard
1 tsp. paprika
1 cup apple cider vinegar
1 cup orange juice
1 tsp. salt

1. Sprinkle both sides of brisket with garlic powder, onion powder, and celery salt. Sprinkle liquid smoke on both sides.
2. Place in large bowl or roaster. Refrigerate overnight, tightly covered.
3. In morning, drain meat. Return meat to pan.
4. Sprinkle with Worcestershire sauce.
5. Bake covered at 225°F for 3–4 hours, or until meat thermometer registers 175°F.
6. While brisket is roasting, prepare barbecue sauce by combining all ingredients in saucepan.
7. Cook uncovered, stirring occasionally, until sauce comes to a boil.
8. Continue simmering for 30 minutes, or until sauce thickens and reduces down.
9. When time is up on roast, turn off oven, but keep meat in oven for 30 more minutes.
10. Slice brisket and serve with barbecue sauce alongside or spooned over meat.

Korean Beef

Hope Comerford, Clinton Township, MI

Makes 8–10 servings

Prep. Time: 8–10 minutes ❧ *Cooking Time: 70 minutes*

1 medium onion
1 McIntosh apple, peeled, cored
5 cloves garlic
¼ cup rice vinegar
1 tsp. gluten-free hot sauce
2 Tbsp. low-sodium gluten-free soy sauce
1 Tbsp. ginger
1 Tbsp. chili powder
¼ tsp. red pepper flakes
3 Tbsp. brown sugar
1 cup ketchup
2–3-lb. chuck roast
1 cup beef broth

1. In a food processor, puree the onion, apple, and garlic. Pour this mixture in a bowl and mix it with the rice vinegar, hot sauce, soy sauce, ginger, chili powder, red pepper flakes, brown sugar, and ketchup.

2. Place the pork roast into the bottom of the inner pot of the Instant Pot. Pour the sauce over the top and turn it so it's covered on all sides. Add the beef broth.

3. Secure the lid and set the vent to sealing. Manually set the cook time for 70 minutes on high pressure.

4. When cook time is up, let the pressure release naturally, then remove lid when the pin drops.

5. Remove the chuck roast and shred it between 2 forks. Return the shredded pork to the inner pot and mix it through the sauce.

Serving suggestion:

Serve over brown rice or quinoa with a side of bok choi sautéed in toasted sesame seed oil and red pepper flakes.

Veggie and Beef Stir-Fry

Margaret H. Moffitt, Middleton, TN

Makes 4 servings

Prep. Time: 15–20 minutes · *Cooking Time: 30–35 minutes*

¼ lb. beef tenderloin
2 tsp. olive oil
1 onion, chopped coarsely
1 small zucchini, chopped coarsely
3 cups coarsely chopped broccoli florets
½ small yellow squash, chopped coarsely
½ cup uncooked brown rice
1 cup water
1 tsp. low-sodium teriyaki sauce

1. Cut beef into ¼-inch-wide strips.
2. In a good-sized skillet, stir-fry beef in 2 tsp. olive oil just until no longer pink, about 2 minutes.
3. Add onion and other vegetables. Stir-fry until tender-crisp, about 5–7 minutes.
4. To cook rice, place rice and water in a saucepan. Cover, and bring to a boil. Adjust heat so that mixture simmers, covered. Cook rice until tender, about 20–25 minutes.
5. Just before serving over rice, add teriyaki sauce to beef and vegetables.

Beef in Noodles

Hope Comerford, Clinton Township, MI

Makes 4–6 servings

Prep. Time: 10 minutes ✿ *Cooking Time: 38–40 minutes*

- 1 Tbsp. butter
- 1½ lb. stew beef
- ½ tsp. salt
- ¼ tsp. pepper
- 6 cups beef broth, *divided*
- 1 tsp. garlic powder
- 1 tsp. onion powder
- 1 Tbsp. Worcestershire sauce
- 1 tsp. low-sodium soy sauce
- ½ cup cornstarch
- ½ cup cold water
- 24 oz. dry egg noodles

1. Set the Instant Pot to the Sauté function and let it get hot.
2. Melt the butter, then immediately add the beef, season with the salt and pepper, and brown on all sides.
3. Add 1 cup of the broth and deglaze the pot, scraping up any stuck-on bits. Press Cancel.
4. Add the remaining broth, garlic powder, onion powder, Worcestershire sauce, and soy sauce.
5. Secure the lid and set the vent to sealing. Manually set the cook time for 28 minutes on high pressure.
6. When cook time is up, manually release the pressure.
7. When the pin drops, remove the lid. In a small bowl, mix the cornstarch and water, then add it into the pot, stirring.
8. Stir in the egg noodles and switch the Instant Pot to the Sauté function once again. Place the lid on the pot and allow the noodles to simmer for 6–8 minutes, or until tender.

Flavorful Beef Stroganoff

Susan Guarneri, Three Lakes, WI

Makes 6 servings

Prep. Time: 25 minutes  *Cooking Time: 1 hour 20 minutes*

2 lb. boneless chuck
¼ cup flour
1 tsp. salt
2 Tbsp. butter
1 medium-sized onion, chopped
1 clove garlic, crushed
10¾-oz. can cream of mushroom soup
½ tsp. cinnamon
¼ tsp. allspice
1 cup water
4-oz. can sliced mushrooms, undrained
1 pt. sour cream

1. Cut chuck in strips ½-inch thick.
2. Mix flour and salt. Dredge meat in flour/salt mixture.
3. Melt butter in large skillet. Brown flour-coated meat in butter over high heat. Stir often so that meat browns on all sides.
4. When meat is browned, turn down heat and add onion, garlic, soup, cinnamon, allspice, and water.
5. Cover and simmer 1 hour.
6. Reduce heat and stir in mushrooms and sour cream. Do not allow to boil, but simmer, covered, until heated through. Serve over egg noodles.

Convenient Slow-Cooker Lasagna

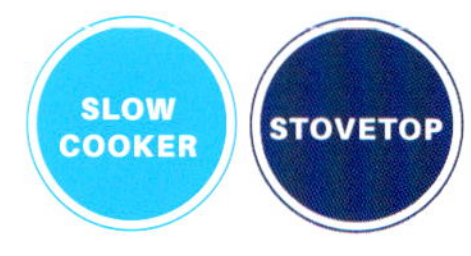

Rachel Yoder, Middlebury, IN

Makes 6–8 servings

Prep. Time: 30–45 minutes · *Cooking Time: 4 hours* · *Ideal slow-cooker size: 6-qt.*

- 1 lb. extra-lean ground beef
- 29-oz. can tomato sauce
- 8-oz. pkg. dry lasagna noodles, *divided*
- 4 cups shredded low-fat mozzarella cheese
- 1½ cups low-fat cottage cheese

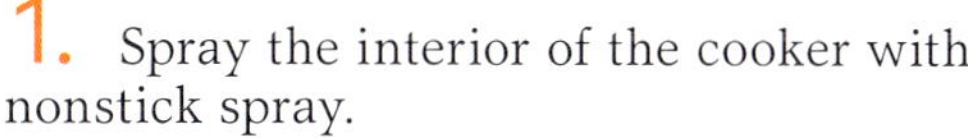

1. Spray the interior of the cooker with nonstick spray.
2. Brown the ground beef in a large nonstick skillet. Drain off drippings.
3. Stir in tomato sauce. Mix well.
4. Spread one-fourth of the meat sauce on the bottom of the slow cooker.
5. Arrange ⅓ of the uncooked noodles over the sauce. If you wish, break them up so they fit better.
6. Combine the cheeses in a bowl. Spoon ⅓ of the cheeses over the noodles.
7. Repeat these layers twice.
8. Top with remaining meat sauce.
9. Cover and cook on Low 4 hours.

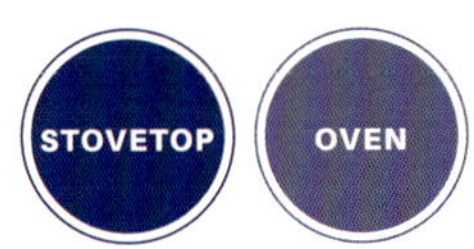

Lasagna

Colleen Heatwole, Burton, MI

Makes 8–12 servings

Prep. Time: 45 minutes   *Baking Time: 30 minutes*

1 lb. ground beef
1 clove garlic, minced
1 scant Tbsp. basil
¾ tsp. salt
28- to 32-oz. can stewed tomatoes, or 28-oz. jar pasta sauce
6-oz. can tomato paste
½ tsp. oregano
10 oz. dry lasagna noodles, *divided*
3 cups cottage cheese
½ cup grated Parmesan cheese
1 lb. mozzarella cheese, grated
2 Tbsp. parsley flakes
2 eggs, beaten
½ tsp. pepper

1. Brown beef slowly in stockpot. Stir frequently to break up clumps. Pour off drippings.
2. Stir in garlic, basil, salt, tomatoes or pasta sauce, tomato paste, and oregano. Mix well.
3. Simmer, uncovered, 30 minutes.
4. Meanwhile, cook pasta al dente, according to package directions. Drain well.
5. In large bowl, combine cottage cheese, Parmesan cheese, mozzarella cheese, parsley flakes, beaten eggs, and pepper.
6. Place half the noodles in greased 9 × 13-inch baking dish.
7. Cover with half the meat sauce.
8. Top with half the cheese mixture.
9. Repeat layers, ending with cheese mixture.
10. Bake at 375°F for 30 minutes, or until bubbly and heated through.

Tip:

You can assemble this lasagna ahead of time through Step 9. Cover and refrigerate. When ready to bake, allow 15 minutes longer in oven, or cover and bake at 200°F for 2 hours if baking during church for a noon potluck.

Variation:

Instead of ground beef, use ½ lb. bulk hot Italian sausage. Brown it as instructed for ground beef and drain off drippings.

—Monica Leaman Kehr, Portland, MI

Shepherd's Pie

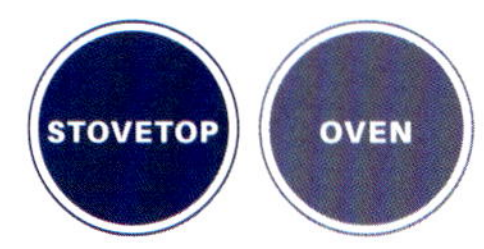

Judi Manos, West Islip, NY

Makes 6 servings

Prep. Time: 15 minutes · *Cooking/Baking Time: 50 minutes*

- 1¼ lb. red potatoes, unpeeled and cut in chunks
- 3 cloves garlic
- 1 lb. 95%-lean ground beef
- 2 Tbsp. flour
- 4 cups fresh vegetables of your choice (for example, carrots, corn, green beans, peas)
- ¾ cup beef broth, canned, or boxed, or your own homemade
- 2 Tbsp. ketchup
- ¾ cup fat-free sour cream
- ½ cup shredded reduced-fat sharp cheddar cheese, *divided*

1. In saucepan, cook potatoes and garlic in 1½ inches boiling water for 20 minutes, or until potatoes are tender.
2. Meanwhile, brown beef in large nonstick skillet.
3. Stir in flour. Cook 1 minute.
4. Stir in vegetables, broth, and ketchup. Cover. Cook 10 minutes, stirring frequently.
5. Drain cooked potatoes and garlic. Return to their pan.
6. Stir in sour cream. Mash until potatoes are smooth and mixture is well blended.
7. Stir ¼ cup cheddar cheese into mashed potatoes.
8. Spoon meat mixture into well-greased 8 × 8-inch baking dish.
9. Cover with mashed potatoes.
10. Bake at 375°F for 18 minutes.
11. Top with remaining cheddar cheese. Bake 2 minutes more, or until cheese is melted.

Variation:

If you don't have access to fresh vegetables, use leftovers from your fridge or frozen ones.

Baked Rice Moussaka

Rhoda Atzeff, Harrisburg, PA

Makes 12 servings, ½ cup per serving

Prep. Time: 30 minutes · *Baking/Cooking Time: 1 hour 20 minutes*

1½ lb. round steak, minced
1 Tbsp. canola oil
¼ cup chopped green pepper
½ cup chopped onion
1 clove garlic, minced
½ cup uncooked rice
1 cup stewed tomatoes
1 tsp. salt
½ tsp. pepper
½ tsp. paprika
½ tsp. dry mint
2 cups hot water
3 eggs
Juice of ½ lemon

1. In a saucepan, brown meat with canola oil. Add green pepper, onion, garlic, rice, tomatoes, and seasonings. Sauté for 5 minutes.

2. Add water and mix well. Pour into baking dish.

3. Beat eggs well and stir in lemon juice. Pour over meat mixture.

4. Bake at 350°F for 1 hour.

Stuffed Bell Peppers

Mary Puterbaugh, Elwood, IN

Makes 8 servings

Prep. Time: 20 minutes ❧ *Cooking Time: 5–11 hours* ❧ *Ideal slow-cooker size: 6- to 7-qt.*

2 lb. extra-lean ground beef, lightly browned
1 large onion, chopped
1 cup cooked brown rice
2 eggs, beaten
½ cup nonfat milk
½ cup ketchup
Dash hot pepper sauce
2 tsp. sea salt
½ tsp. pepper
8 large bell peppers, capped and seeded

1. Combine all ingredients except peppers. Gently pack mixture into peppers. Place in greased slow cooker.

2. Cover. Cook on Low 9–11 hours, or on High 5–6 hours.

Un-Stuffed Peppers

Pat Bechtel, Dillsburg, PA
Sharon Miller, Holmesville, OH

Makes 6 servings

Prep. Time: 10–12 minutes *Cooking Time: 25 minutes*

- 1 lb. ground beef
- 10-oz. jar spaghetti sauce
- 2 Tbsp. barbecue sauce, *optional*
- 2 large greenpeppers, coarsely chopped (3–4 cups)
- 1¼ cups water
- 1 cup instant rice

1. In a 12-inch nonstick skillet, brown ground beef. Drain off drippings.

2. Stir in all remaining ingredients. Bring to a boil over high heat.

3. Reduce heat to medium-low and cook, covered, for 20 minutes, or until liquid is absorbed and rice is tender.

Variation:

Instead of spaghetti sauce and water, substitute 4 cups tomato juice or V8 juice.

—Sharon Miller, Holmesville, OH

Italian Stuffed Cabbage

Maxine "Meme" Phaneuf, Washington Township, MI
Hope Comerford, Clinton Township, MI

Makes 6–8 servings

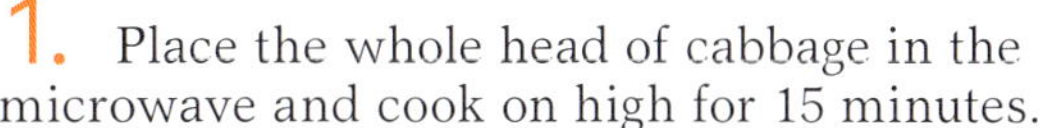

1 whole head of green cabbage
1 lb. ground beef, browned and drained
1 cup uncooked white rice
1 large onion, chopped
½ cup finely chopped Italian parsley
2 large tomatoes, chopped
3 cloves garlic, finely chopped
1 tsp. salt
¼ tsp. pepper
¼ cup olive oil
½ cup lemon juice

1. Place the whole head of cabbage in the microwave and cook on high for 15 minutes.
2. In a bowl, mix the browned ground beef, rice, onion, parsley, tomatoes, garlic, salt, pepper, olive oil, and lemon juice.
3. When the time is up on the microwave, let the cabbage cool slightly, then peel the leaves off of the core.
4. Thin the vein on each leaf.
5. Stuff each leaf with about 2–3 Tbsp. of the stuffing mixture; tuck the leaves and roll them.
6. Place each cabbage roll into the bottom of a stockpot. Make sure they're packed in very tightly. When all the leaves are stuffed and stuffed into the pot, place a lid inside the pot to weigh them down.
7. Pour water into the pot, just enough to cover the leaves.
8. Cover and cook on medium heat for 25 minutes.
9. Simmer on low heat for an additional 25 minutes.

Reuben Casserole

Joleen Albrecht, Gladstone, MI

Makes 8–10 servings

Prep. Time: 25 minutes · *Baking Time: 25 minutes*

- 1½ cups Thousand Island salad dressing
- 1 cup sour cream
- 1 Tbsp. minced onion
- 12 slices dark rye bread, cubed, *divided*
- 1 lb. sauerkraut, drained
- 1½ lb. corned beef, sliced and cut into bite-sized pieces
- 2 cups shredded Swiss cheese
- ¼ cup melted butter or margarine

1. In a mixing bowl, stir together dressing, sour cream, and onion. Set aside.
2. Arrange bread cubes in a greased 9 × 13-inch baking dish, setting aside approximately 1 cup cubes for the top.
3. Top the bread with a layer of sauerkraut, followed by a layer of corned beef.
4. Spread dressing mixture over corned beef. Sprinkle with Swiss cheese.
5. Top with remaining bread cubes. Drizzle with melted butter.
6. Cover and bake at 350°F for 15 minutes. Uncover and continue baking for about 10 minutes or until bubbly.

Goulash

Janie Steele, Moore, OK

Makes 8–10 servings

Prep. Time: 15 minutes *Cooking Time: 6 hours* *Ideal slow-cooker size: 5-qt.*

1 lb. extra-lean ground beef
1 pkg. low-sodium taco seasoning
2 cups water
15-oz. can low-sodium diced tomatoes
15-oz. can low-sodium tomato sauce
15-oz. can whole-kernel corn, drained
Salt and pepper to taste
2 cups dry elbow macaroni

1. Brown meat in a skillet and drain.

2. Mix remaining ingredients except the macaroni together and pour into slow cooker.

3. Add elbow macaroni, then mix.

4. Cover and cook 6 hours on Low.

Sloppy Joes

Hope Comerford, Clinton Township, MI

Makes 15–18 servings

Prep. Time: 25 minutes · *Cooking Time: 6–7 hours* · *Ideal slow-cooker size: 6-qt.*

1½ lb. extra-lean ground beef
16 oz. ground turkey sausage
½ large red onion, chopped
½ green bell pepper, chopped
8-oz. can low-sodium tomato sauce
½ cup water
½ cup ketchup
¼ cup tightly packed brown sugar
2 Tbsp. apple cider vinegar
2 Tbsp. yellow mustard
1 Tbsp. Worcestershire sauce
1 Tbsp. chili powder
1 tsp. garlic powder
1 tsp. onion powder
¼ tsp. salt
¼ tsp. pepper

1. Brown the ground beef and sausage in a pan. Drain all grease.
2. While the beef and sausage are cooking, mix the remaining ingredients in the crock.
3. Add the cooked beef and sausage to the crock and mix.
4. Cover and cook on Low for 6–7 hours.

Serving suggestion:

Serve on hamburger buns.

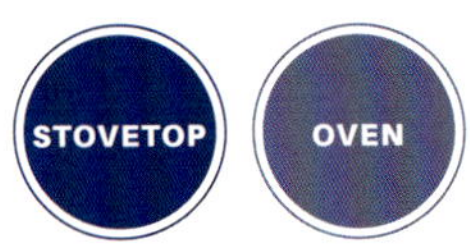

Impossible Taco Pie

Esther J. Mast, Lancaster, PA

Makes 6–8 servings

Prep. Time: 15–20 minutes · *Baking Time: 43–45 minutes*

- 1 lb. ground beef
- ½ cup chopped onion
- 1 pkg. taco seasoning mix
- 4 eggs
- 2 cups milk
- 1⅓ cups baking mix
- 2 fresh tomatoes, sliced or chopped
- 4 oz. shredded cheddar cheese
- 2 cups chopped lettuce
- 2 cups fresh, chopped tomatoes
- ½ cup sour cream

1. Brown beef and onion together in nonstick skillet. Drain off drippings.
2. Stir in taco seasoning.
3. Spread mixture in greased 10-inch pie plate.
4. In mixing bowl, beat eggs. Add milk and baking mix and beat until smooth.
5. Pour into plate over top of meat.
6. Bake at 400°F for 35 minutes.
7. Arrange 2 sliced or chopped tomatoes on top. Sprinkle cheese on top.
8. Bake 8–10 minutes more until cheese melts.
9. Serve with lettuce, chopped tomatoes, and sour cream for those at your table to add as they wish.

Variation:

If you wish, add 15-oz. can kidney beans, drained, to Step 2.

—Fran Sauder, Mount Joy, PA

Favorite Enchilada Casserole

Janice Muller, Derwood, MD

Makes 6–8 servings

Prep. Time: 20 minutes · *Baking Time: 30 minutes*

- 1 lb. ground beef, or ground turkey
- 2 onions, chopped
- 1 red or green bell pepper, chopped
- 10½-oz. can beef gravy
- 10½-oz. can beef consommé
- 10½-oz. can mild enchilada sauce
- 7-oz. can pitted black olives, *divided*
- 12 corn tortillas, *divided*
- 1¾ lb. longhorn cheddar cheese, shredded, *divided*

1. In large nonstick skillet, brown ground meat with onions and bell pepper, until meat is no longer pink and vegetables are just-tender. Drain off any drippings.
2. In saucepan, heat gravy, consommé, and enchilada sauce together.
3. Into a well-greased 9 × 13-inch baking pan, layer half the tortillas, half the beef mixture, half the olives, half the sauce, and half the cheese.
4. Repeat layers.
5. Bake at 350°F for 30 minutes.

Burritos

Betty L. Moore, Plano, IL

Makes 10 servings

Prep. Time: 15–20 minutes · *Baking Time: 30–40 minutes*

1 lb. ground beef
1 small green pepper, diced
1 small onion, diced
4-oz. can sliced mushrooms, drained
2 tsp., or 1 pkg., taco seasoning
15-oz. can refried beans
10¾-oz. can cream of mushroom soup
1 pint sour cream
10 flour tortillas
8-oz. shredded cheddar cheese

1. In nonstick skillet, brown ground beef, pepper, and onion. Stir frequently to break up clumps. Drain, if needed.
2. Add mushrooms, taco seasoning, and refried beans. Mix well.
3. Combine soup and sour cream in a bowl.
4. Spoon half of soup/sour cream blend in greased 9 × 13-inch baking pan.
5. Divide meat mixture evenly between tortillas. Roll up. Place rolled burritos in baking pan.
6. Cover with remaining sauce. Sprinkle with cheese.
7. Bake at 350°F for 30–40 minutes, or until bubbly and lightly browned.

Pizza Cups

Barbara Smith, Bedford, PA

Makes 6 servings

¾ lb. ground beef
6-oz. can tomato paste
1 Tbsp. minced onion
½ tsp. salt
1 tsp. Italian seasoning
1 can refrigerated biscuits
½–¾ cup shredded mozzarella cheese

1. In skillet, brown beef. Drain.
2. Stir in tomato paste, onion, and seasonings.
3. Cook over low heat for 5 minutes, stirring frequently. Mixture will thicken.
4. Meanwhile, place biscuits in greased muffin tins. Press them in so they cover the bottom and sides of each cup.
5. Spoon about ¼ cup meat mixture into each biscuit-lined cup. Sprinkle with cheese.
6. Bake at 400°F for 12–15 minutes, or until brown.

Upside-Down Pizza

Julia Rohrer, Aaronsburg, PA
Janet L. Roggie, Lowville, NY

Makes 10 servings (2½ × 4½-inch rectangle)

Prep. Time: 20–30 minutes · *Baking Time: 25–30 minutes*

14 oz. 95%-lean ground beef
1 chopped onion
1 medium red or green bell pepper, chopped
1 tsp. dry basil
1 tsp. dry oregano
2 cups pizza or spaghetti sauce
¼ lb. fresh mushrooms, chopped, or 4-oz. can chopped mushrooms, drained
1 cup grated part-skim mozzarella cheese

Batter:

¾ cup egg substitute
1½ cups fat-free milk
1½ Tbsp. oil
½ tsp. salt
1 tsp. baking soda
1¾ cups flour
Sprinkle dry oregano
Sprinkle grated Parmesan cheese

1. Brown meat with onion and pepper in large nonstick skillet.
2. Stir in seasonings, sauce, and mushrooms. Simmer 5–8 minutes.
3. Place in well-greased 9 × 13-inch baking pan.
4. Cover with grated cheese.
5. Prepare batter by beating egg substitute, milk, and oil together in good-sized mixing bowl.
6. Add salt, baking soda, and flour. Stir just until mixed.
7. Pour over cheese-meat mixture. Do not stir.
8. Sprinkle with oregano and Parmesan cheese.
9. Bake at 400°F for 25–30 minutes or until toothpick inserted in center of dough comes out clean.

Meatless & Seafood

Mjadra (Lentils and Rice)

Hope Comerford, Clinton Township, MI

Makes 4–6 servings

Prep. Time: 1 hour 20 minutes ⁂ *Cooking Time: 20–25 minutes*

½ cup olive oil
2 large sweet onions, chopped
1 cup dry lentils
4 cups water
¼ cup lemon juice
⅛ tsp. pepper
1 tsp. salt
1 cup uncooked white rice

1. Heat the olive oil over medium-high heat. Add the onions and let brown lightly. Reduce the heat to low and cover. Let the onions caramelize for at least 1 hour.

2. Rinse the lentils then add them with the 4 cups fresh water to a saucepan. Bring to a boil and cook for 15 minutes.

3. When the onions are done, mix them with the cooked lentils, lemon juice, pepper, salt, and uncooked white rice.

4. Cover and cook for 20–25 minutes, or until the rice and lentils are fluffy.

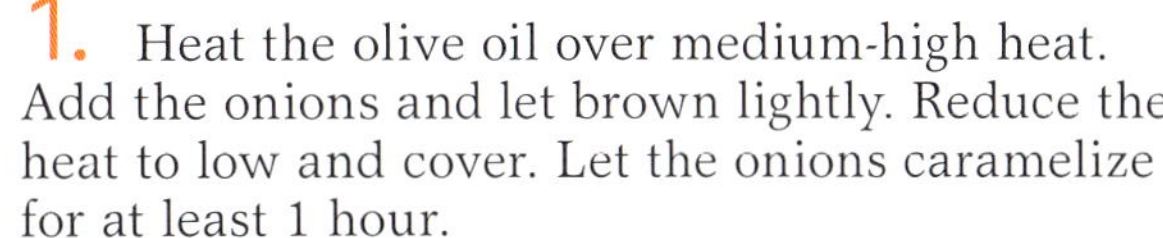

Serving suggestion:

Serve with pita bread or on a bed of lettuce.

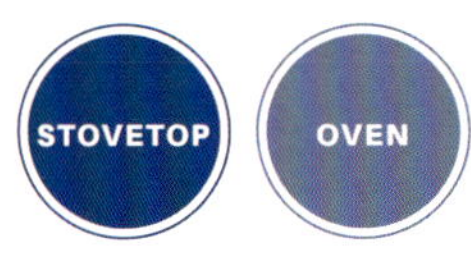

Vegetarian Black Bean Burritos

Maricarol Magill, Freehold, NJ

Makes 8 burritos

Prep. Time: 10 minutes ⁂ *Cooking/Baking Time: 40 minutes*

1¼ cups water
1 Tbsp. butter
½ cup long-grain rice
½ tsp. salt
8 (10-inch) flour tortillas
10-oz. pkg. frozen corn
15-oz. can spicy black-bean chili
8-oz. can tomato sauce
Shredded cheddar, Monterey Jack, or pepper Jack cheese

1. In a medium-sized saucepan, bring water and butter to a boil.

2. Stir in rice and salt. Cover. Simmer over low heat until rice is cooked, about 20 minutes.

3. Meanwhile, wrap tortillas in foil. Heat oven to 350°F and then heat tortillas until warm, about 15 minutes.

4. When rice is done, stir in corn, black-bean chili, and tomato sauce. Heat to boiling over medium-high heat. Boil one minute.

5. Assemble burritos by spooning rice mixture onto tortillas. Top with cheese of your choice. Fold in tops of tortillas and roll up.

Eggplant Parmesan

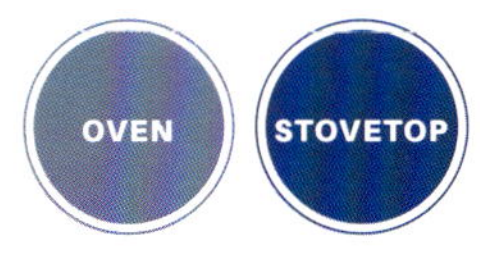

Mary Ann Bowman, East Earl, PA

Makes 6 main-dish servings

Prep. Time: 15 minutes · *Broiling/Baking Time: 40–45 minutes*

- 1 medium eggplant, unpeeled
- 2 Tbsp. olive oil, *divided*
- 1 cup breadcrumbs
- ½ tsp. dry basil
- ¾ cup grated Parmesan cheese, *divided*
- 2 Tbsp. chopped parsley
- ⅛ tsp. pepper
- 1 tsp. dry oregano
- 6 tomatoes, chopped
- 2 green bell peppers, chopped
- 2 onions, chopped
- 1 clove garlic, chopped
- 2 Tbsp. tomato paste
- 1 cup grated Swiss cheese

1. Preheat oven to broil.
2. Cut eggplant into 6 slices, each ½-inch thick.
3. Place slices on cookie sheet. Brush with half the olive oil.
4. Broil 5 minutes, or until golden.
5. Turn slices. Brush other sides with remaining oil.
6. Return to broiler and brown second sides.
7. Place browned eggplant in lightly greased 9 × 13-inch baking pan, sprayed generously with nonstick cooking spray.
8. Mix together breadcrumbs, basil, ½ cup Parmesan cheese, parsley, pepper, and oregano in a small bowl. Sprinkle over eggplant.
9. Combine in saucepan tomatoes, peppers, onions, garlic, and tomato paste. Simmer uncovered about 20 minutes.
10. Spread on top of crumb mixture.
11. Top with Swiss cheese and ¼ cup Parmesan cheese.
12. Bake uncovered at 375°F for 10–15 minutes.

Tip:

You can make this ahead and refrigerate it until you're ready to heat and serve it.

Super Creamy Macaroni and Cheese

Jean Butzer, Batavia, NY
Arlene Leaman Kliewer, Lakewood, CO
Esther Burkholder, Millerstown, PA
Hazel Lightcap Propst, Oxford, PA
Karla Baer, North Lima, OH

Makes 8–10 servings

Prep. Time: 5–10 minutes ❧ *Baking Time: 1 hour 20 minutes*

1 lb. dry elbow macaroni
4 cups shredded cheddar cheese, or ½ lb. cubed Velveeta cheese
2 (10¾-oz.) cans cheddar cheese, or cream of celery, soup
3½ cups milk
1½ cups cooked ham, chopped, *optional*
1 tsp. salt, *optional*
¼ tsp. pepper, *optional*

1. Combine all ingredients in a buttered 3-qt. casserole or baking dish.
2. Cover and bake at 350°F for 1 hour.
3. Stir up from bottom.
4. Bake uncovered an additional 20 minutes.

Pasta Primavera

Marcia S. Myer, Manheim, PA

Makes 6 main-dish servings

Prep. Time: 20–30 minutes *Cooking Time: 25 minutes*

3 cups broccoli florets, cut bite-sized
½ lb. fresh mushrooms, quartered
2 small zucchini, sliced into ¼-inch-thick rounds
1 Tbsp. olive oil
1–3 cloves garlic, minced, according to your taste preference
1 pt. cherry tomatoes, halved
8-oz. pkg. whole-grain fettuccine
Black pepper to taste
3 Tbsp. grated reduced-fat Parmesan cheese

Sauce:

¾ cup skim milk
1 Tbsp. olive oil
⅔ cup part-skim ricotta cheese
¼ cup grated reduced-fat Parmesan cheese
2 Tbsp. chopped fresh basil, or 1 Tbsp. dry basil
2 tsp. dry sherry

1. In large microwave-safe bowl, layer in broccoli, mushrooms, and zucchini. Cover bowl and microwave on High for 2 minutes.

2. Stir. Cover and cook another 2 minutes on High, or until tender-crisp.

3. In nonstick skillet, heat olive oil. Add garlic and sauté for 1 minute. Add tomatoes and sauté for 2 minutes, or until tomatoes are slightly cooked but not wilted.

4. Cook fettuccine as directed with no salt. Drain. Keep warm.

5. Prepare sauce by combining milk, oil, ricotta cheese, Parmesan cheese, basil, and sherry in a blender.

6. Process until smooth. Heat sauce until warm, on stove or in microwave.

7. In large serving bowl, toss drained pasta, vegetables, and sauce.

8. Garnish with black pepper and 3 Tbsp. grated Parmesan cheese.

Meatless Ziti

Hope Comerford, Clinton Township, MI

Makes 8 servings

Prep. Time: 10 minutes ♣ *Cooking Time: 3 minutes*

- 1 Tbsp. olive oil
- 1 small onion, chopped
- 3 cups water, *divided*
- 15-oz. can crushed tomatoes
- 8-oz. can tomato sauce
- 1½ tsp. Italian seasoning
- 1 tsp. garlic powder
- 1 tsp. onion powder
- 1 tsp. sea salt
- ¼ tsp. pepper
- 12 oz. ziti
- 1–2 cups shredded mozzarella cheese

1. Set the Instant Pot to the Sauté function and heat the olive oil.

2. When the oil is hot, sauté the onion for 3 to 5 minutes, or until translucent.

3. Pour in 1 cup of the water and scrape any bits from the bottom of the inner pot with a wooden spoon or spatula.

4. In a bowl, mix the crushed tomatoes, tomato sauce, Italian seasoning, garlic powder, onion powder, sea salt, and pepper. Pour 1 cup of this in the inner pot, add remaining 2 cups water, and stir.

5. Pour in the ziti. Press it down so it's in there evenly, but do not stir.

6. Pour the remaining pasta sauce evenly over the top. Again, do not stir.

7. Secure the lid and set the vent to sealing. Manually set the cook time for 3 minutes.

8. When the cook time is over, let the pressure release naturally for 10 minutes, then manually release the remaining pressure.

9. When the pin drops, remove the lid and stir in the shredded mozzarella. This will thicken as it sits a bit.

Fresh Veggie Lasagna

Deanne Gingrich, Lancaster, PA

Makes 4–6 servings

Prep. Time: 30 minutes ❧ *Cooking Time: 4 hours* ❧ *Ideal slow-cooker size: 4- or 5-qt.*

- 1½ cups shredded low-fat mozzarella cheese
- ½ cup low-fat ricotta cheese
- ⅓ cup grated Parmesan cheese
- 1 egg, lightly beaten
- 1 tsp. dry oregano
- ¼ tsp. garlic powder
- 3 cups marinara sauce, *divided*
- 1 medium zucchini, diced, *divided*
- 4 dry lasagna noodles
- 4 cups fresh baby spinach, *divided*
- 1 cup fresh mushrooms, sliced, *divided*

1. Grease interior of slow-cooker crock.
2. In a bowl, mix the mozzarella, ricotta, and Parmesan cheeses, egg, oregano, and garlic powder. Set aside.
3. Spread ½ cup marinara sauce in crock.
4. Sprinkle with half the zucchini.
5. Spoon ⅓ of cheese mixture over zucchini.
6. Break 2 noodles into large pieces to cover cheese layer.
7. Spread ½ cup marinara over the noodles.
8. Top with half the spinach and then half the mushrooms.
9. Repeat layers, ending with cheese mixture, and then sauce. Press layers down firmly.
10. Cover and cook on Low for 4 hours, or until vegetables are as tender as you like them and noodles are fully cooked.
11. Let stand 15 minutes so lasagna can firm up before serving.

Tuna Noodle Casserole

Carol Lenz, Little Chute, WI

Rosemarie Fitzgerald, Gibsonia, PA

Makes 6–8 servings

Prep. Time: 15 minutes · *Baking Time: 30–45 minutes*

2 cups dry elbow macaroni
2 (6-oz.) cans tuna, packed in water
2 (10¾-oz.) cans mushroom soup
2 cups shredded cheddar cheese
Salt and pepper to taste
1 cup frozen peas, *optional*
¾ cup cornflake crumbs, *optional*

1. Cook macaroni according to package directions. Drain. Place cooked pasta in a large mixing bowl.

2. Stir in tuna, soup, cheese, salt and pepper, and peas if you wish. Stir together gently until well mixed.

3. Place in lightly greased 2-qt. casserole. Top with cornflake crumbs if you wish.

4. Bake uncovered at 350°F for 30–45 minutes, or until heated through and bubbly.

Desserts

Vanilla Pudding

Rhonda Freed, Croghan, NY

Makes 8–10 servings

Prep. Time: 15 minutes · *Cooking Time: 25 minutes* · *Chilling Time: 2–4 hours*

8 cups whole milk, *divided*
¾ cup cornstarch
1¼ cups sugar
2 eggs
2 tsp. vanilla extract

Note:

I am at least the fourth generation (that I know of and remember) to make this recipe. My mom adapted it for the microwave, which saves standing and stirring over a double boiler on a hot stovetop!

1. In a 3- or 4-qt. microwave-safe bowl, heat 6 cups milk in microwave on High until scalded, approximately 8–10 minutes.
2. Meanwhile, blend remaining milk, the cornstarch, sugar, and eggs in blender until smooth.
3. Whisk blended ingredients into scalded milk.
4. Microwave on High for 5 minutes. Remove carefully with potholders and mix with whisk.
5. Microwave on High for 4 minutes and stir. Decrease cooking time by a minute each time until the pudding is a bit thinner than you want. (It will continue to thicken as it cools.)
6. Remove from microwave. Stir in vanilla.
7. While still hot, cover with plastic wrap, pressing plastic against the surface of the pudding to prevent a skin from forming.

Variation:

Pour the finished pudding into ice pop molds. Freeze for pudding pops.

Buttery Rice Pudding

Janie Steele, Moore, OK

Makes 6–8 servings

Prep. Time: 5 minutes ♣ *Cooking Time: 14 minutes*

1½ Tbsp. butter
1 cup uncooked rice
½ cup sugar
1 cup water
2 cups milk (2% works best)
1 egg
¼ cup evaporated milk
½ tsp. vanilla extract
½ tsp. almond extract, *optional*
Nutmeg, *optional*
Cinnamon, *optional*

1. In the inner pot of the Instant Pot, melt butter using the Sauté setting. Add the rice, sugar, water, and milk, and stir.

2. Secure lid and make sure vent is at sealing. Cook on Manual on high pressure for 14 minutes. Let the pressure release naturally when cook time is up.

3. In a bowl whisk together the egg and evaporated milk.

4. Take a spoon of rice mixture and add slowly to egg mixture.

5. Return all to the inner pot and stir in the vanilla and optional almond extract.

6. Use the Sauté function and bring mixture to bubble for 30–60 seconds.

7. Stir slowly so it does not stick to the pot.

8. Use nutmeg or cinnamon to garnish if desired.

Cheesecake

Dot Hess, Willow Street, PA

Makes 12 servings

Prep. Time: 30 minutes · *Baking Time: 1 hour 10 minutes* · *Chilling Time: 3 hours*

Crust:

1½ cups crushed graham crackers
¼ cup sugar
½ stick (4 Tbsp.) butter, softened

Filling:

3 (8-oz.) pkgs. cream cheese, softened
5 eggs
1 cup sugar
1½ tsp. vanilla extract

Topping:

1½ pts. sour cream
⅓ cup sugar
1½ tsp. vanilla extract

1. Combine graham crackers, sugar, and butter. Press into bottom of 9-inch springform pan.
2. Beat cream cheese well with mixer. Add eggs, one at a time, mixing well after each one.
3. Add sugar and vanilla. Mix well.
4. Pour gently over prepared crust.
5. Bake at 300°F for 1 hour. Cool 5 minutes. Do not turn off oven.
6. As the cake cools, mix sour cream, sugar, and vanilla.
7. Spread topping on cake and bake 5 minutes more.
8. Chill for at least 3 hours before serving.

Variation:

Omit crust. Bake at 350°F for 35 minutes and proceed with topping.

—Renee Hankins, Narvon, PA

Whoopie Pie Cake

Sheila Plock, Boalsburg, PA

Makes 20–24 servings

Prep. Time: 20 minutes ❧ *Cooking/Baking Time: 20–25 minutes* ❧ *Cooling Time: 1 hour*

1 box chocolate cake mix

1 extra egg (beyond those needed on box recipe)

Filling:

1 stick (8 Tbsp.) margarine, softened

½ cup shortening

1 cup sugar

Pinch salt

1 tsp. vanilla extract

½ cup milk

4 Tbsp. flour

1. Mix cake mix as directed on package with the addition of one extra egg.
2. Grease one 9 × 13-inch pan. Pour in half the batter.
3. Line another 9 × 13-inch pan with waxed paper on the bottom and up the sides to use as handles after the cake is baked.
4. Pour the other half of the batter in the waxed paper pan.
5. Bake according to package directions, possibly decreasing baking time because the mix is halved per pan. Check for doneness by inserting toothpick near center of cake. If toothpick is clean, cake is done. Cool at least 1 hour.
6. Make the filling by creaming margarine, shortening, sugar, and pinch of salt in a medium mixing bowl.
7. Slowly add vanilla and milk.
8. Add flour, 1 Tbsp. at a time. Beat on high 5 minutes until sugar dissolves.
9. Spread filling on bottom cake layer in greased pan.
10. To make the top layer, lift the other cake out of pan with waxed paper. Remove waxed paper. Place on top of filling.

Upside-Down Chocolate Pudding Cake

Sarah Herr, Goshen, IN

Makes 8 servings

Prep. Time: 15 minutes ✿ *Cooking Time: 2–3 hours* ✿ *Ideal slow-cooker size: 3½-qt.*

1 cup dry all-purpose baking mix

1 cup sugar, *divided*

3 Tbsp. + ⅓ cup unsweetened cocoa powder, *divided*

½ cup milk

1 tsp. vanilla extract

1⅔ cups hot water

1. Spray inside of slow cooker with nonstick cooking spray.

2. In a bowl, mix the baking mix, ½ cup sugar, 3 Tbsp. cocoa powder, milk, and vanilla. Spoon batter evenly into slow cooker.

3. In a clean bowl, mix remaining ½ cup sugar, ⅓ cup cocoa powder, and hot water together. Pour over batter in slow cooker. Do not stir.

4. Cover and cook on High 2–3 hours, or until toothpick inserted in center of cakey part comes out clean.

Tip:

The batter will rise to the top and turn into cake. Underneath will be a rich chocolate pudding.

Fudge Sundae Pie

Deb Martin, Gap, PA

Makes 6 servings

Prep. Time: 30 minutes ❧ *Freezing Time: 2 hours*

¼ cup + 3 Tbsp. light corn syrup, *divided*
2 Tbsp. brown sugar
3 Tbsp. butter or margarine
2½ cups crispy rice cereal
¼ cup peanut butter
¼ cup ice cream fudge sauce
1 qt. vanilla ice cream

1. Combine ¼ cup corn syrup, the brown sugar, and the butter in a medium saucepan.
2. Cook over low heat, stirring occasionally, until mixture begins to boil. Remove from heat.
3. Add the crispy rice cereal, stirring until well coated.
4. Press evenly into a 9-inch pie plate to form crust.
5. Stir together the peanut butter, fudge sauce, and 3 Tbsp. corn syrup.
6. Spread half the peanut butter mixture over the crust. Freeze until firm, 1 hour.
7. Allow the ice cream to soften slightly.
8. Spoon the ice cream into the frozen piecrust; spread evenly. Freeze until firm, 1 hour.
9. Let pie stand at room temperature for 10 minutes before cutting and serving.
10. Warm the other half of the peanut butter mixture and drizzle over the top.

Grandma's Apple Pie

Andrea Zuercher, Lawrence, KS

Makes 8 servings

Prep. Time: 30 minutes ✿ *Baking Time: 45 minutes*

6 cups pared and sliced apples (about 6 medium-sized tart apples; Granny Smith work well)

6-oz. can frozen 100%-juice apple juice concentrate, thawed

1½ Tbsp. cornstarch

1 Tbsp. water

1 tsp. cinnamon

10-inch double pie crust, unbaked

3 Tbsp. butter, *optional*

1. Place sliced apples in saucepan with juice concentrate.
2. Bring to a boil. Reduce heat, and then simmer, covered, for 5 minutes.
3. In a small bowl, dissolve cornstarch in water.
4. Gently stir into the apples.
5. Bring to a boil. Reduce heat. Simmer, covered, for 10–15 minutes. Apples will begin to soften as mixture becomes thickened. Stir occasionally so it does not scorch.
6. Gently stir in cinnamon.
7. Fill bottom pie crust with apples.
8. Dot with butter if you wish.
9. Cover with top crust. Pinch crusts together. With a sharp knife, cut 6–8 steam vents across the top crust.
10. Place pie pan on a baking sheet in case the filling cooks out. Bake at 350°F for about 45 minutes, or until top crust is lightly browned.

Peach Cobbler

Phyllis Good, Lancaster, PA

Makes 8 servings

Prep. Time: 20 minutes · *Cooking Time: 3–4 hours* · *Ideal slow-cooker size: 5-qt.*

- 3–4 cups sliced peaches
- ⅓ cup sugar
- ¼ cup brown sugar
- Dash nutmeg
- Dash cinnamon
- 1 stick (8 Tbsp.) butter
- ½ cup sugar
- ¾ cup flour
- 2 tsp. baking powder
- ¾ cup milk

Serving suggestion:

Serve warm with milk or ice cream.

1. Grease interior of slow-cooker crock.

2. Mix together in a good-sized bowl the peaches, ⅓ cup sugar, brown sugar, nutmeg, and cinnamon. Set aside to macerate.

3. Melt butter, or place in slow-cooker crock turned on High and let it melt there.

4. Meanwhile, stir together remaining ingredients in a bowl—½ cup sugar, flour, baking powder, and milk—until smooth.

5. When butter is melted, make sure it covers the bottom of the crock. Spoon batter evenly over butter in crock, but don't stir.

6. Spoon sugared peaches over batter.

7. Cover. Bake on High 3–4 hours, or until firm in middle and bubbly around the edges.

8. Uncover carefully so condensation from inside of lid doesn't drip on the cobbler. Remove crock from cooker.

Slow-Cooker Berry Cobbler

Wilma Haberkamp, Fairbank, IA
Virginia Graybill, Hershey, PA

Makes 8 servings

Prep. Time: 15–20 minutes · *Cooking Time: 2–2½ hours* · *Ideal slow-cooker size: 5-qt.*

- 1¼ cups all-purpose flour, *divided*
- 2 Tbsp. + 1 cup sugar, *divided*
- 1 tsp. baking powder
- ¼ tsp. ground cinnamon
- 1 egg, lightly beaten
- ¼ cup skim milk
- 2 Tbsp. canola oil
- ⅛ tsp. salt
- 2 cups unsweetened raspberries, fresh, or thawed if frozen, and drained
- 2 cups unsweetened blueberries, fresh, or thawed if frozen, and drained

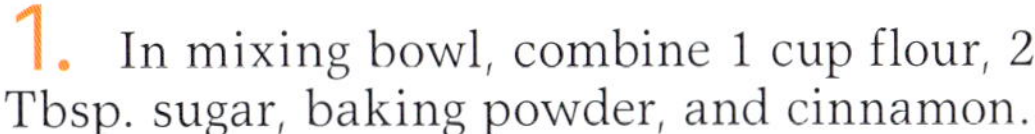

1. In mixing bowl, combine 1 cup flour, 2 Tbsp. sugar, baking powder, and cinnamon.
2. In a separate bowl, combine egg, milk, and oil. Stir into dry ingredients until moistened. Batter will be thick.
3. Spray slow cooker with cooking spray. Spread batter evenly on bottom of slow cooker.
4. In another bowl combine salt, remaining flour, remaining sugar, and berries. Toss to coat berries.
5. Spread berries over batter.
6. Cook on High 2–2½ hours, or until toothpick inserted into cobbler comes out clean.

Pineapple Dessert

Joyce Nolt, Richland, PA

Makes 20 servings

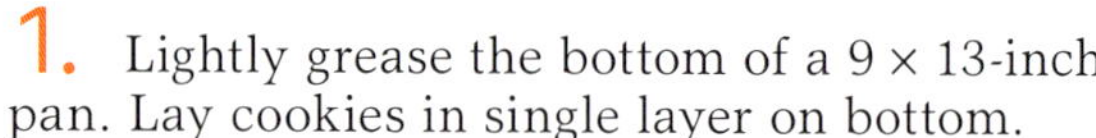

10-oz. shortbread cookies
12-oz. whipped topping
20-oz. crushed pineapple with juice
6-oz. vanilla instant pudding
16-oz. sour cream

1. Lightly grease the bottom of a 9 × 13-inch pan. Lay cookies in single layer on bottom.

2. Mix whipped topping, crushed pineapples with juice, powdered pudding mix, and sour cream.

3. Spread mixture over cookies.

4. Cover. Refrigerate 24 hours.

Recipe & Ingredient Index

D

E

F

G

N

O

P

Q

R

S

T

U

Metric Equivalent Measurements

If you're accustomed to using metric measurements, I don't want you to be inconvenienced by the imperial measurements I use in this book.

Use this handy chart, too, to figure out the size of the slow cooker you'll need for each recipe.

Weight (Dry Ingredients)

1 oz		30 g
4 oz	¼ lb	120 g
8 oz	½ lb	240 g
12 oz	¾ lb	360 g
16 oz	1 lb	480 g
32 oz	2 lb	960 g

Slow-Cooker Sizes

1-quart	0.96 l
2-quart	1.92 l
3-quart	2.88 l
4-quart	3.84 l
5-quart	4.80 l
6-quart	5.76 l
7-quart	6.72 l
8-quart	7.68 l

Volume (Liquid Ingredients)

½ tsp.		2 ml
1 tsp.		5 ml
1 Tbsp.	½ fl oz	15 ml
2 Tbsp.	1 fl oz	30 ml
¼ cup	2 fl oz	60 ml
⅓ cup	3 fl oz	80 ml
½ cup	4 fl oz	120 ml
⅔ cup	5 fl oz	160 ml
¾ cup	6 fl oz	180 ml
1 cup	8 fl oz	240 ml
1 pt	16 fl oz	480 ml
1 qt	32 fl oz	960 ml

Length

¼ in	6 mm
½ in	13 mm
¾ in	19 mm
1 in	25 mm
6 in	15 cm
12 in	30 cm

About the Author

Hope Comerford is a mom, wife, elementary music teacher, blogger, recipe developer, public speaker, Young Living Essential Oils essential oil enthusiast/educator, and published author. In 2013, she was diagnosed with a severe gluten intolerance and since then has spent many hours creating easy, practical, and delicious gluten-free recipes that can be enjoyed by both those who are affected by gluten and those who are not.

Growing up, Hope spent many hours in the kitchen with her Meme (grandmother) and her love for cooking grew from there. While working on her master's degree when her daughter was young, Hope turned to her slow cookers for some salvation and sanity. It was from there she began truly experimenting with recipes and quickly learned she had the ability to get a little more creative in the kitchen and develop her own recipes.

In 2010, Hope started her blog, *A Busy Mom's Slow Cooker Adventures*, to simply share the recipes she was making with her family and friends. She never imagined people all over the world would begin visiting her page and sharing her recipes with others as well. In 2013, Hope self-published her first cookbook, *Slow Cooker Recipes 10 Ingredients or Less and Gluten-Free*, and then later wrote *The Gluten-Free Slow Cooker*.

Hope became the new brand ambassador and author of Fix-It and Forget-It in mid-2016. Since then, she has brought her excitement and creativeness to the Fix-It and Forget-It brand. Through Fix-It and Forget-It, she has written *Welcome Home Family Favorites, Fix-It and Forget-It Slow Cooker Dump Dinners & Desserts, Fix-It and Forget-It Instant Pot Cookbook, Fix-It and Forget-It Freezer Meals, Welcome Weeknight Favorites*, and many more.

Hope lives in the city of Clinton Township, Michigan, near Metro Detroit. She has been happily married to her husband and best friend, Justin, since 2008. Together they have two children, Ella and Gavin, who are her motivation, inspiration, and heart. In her spare time, Hope enjoys traveling, singing, cooking, reading books, spending time with friends and family, and relaxing.